D1172708

BLACK
ON
WHITE

BLACK ON WHITE

A CRITICAL SURVEY OF
WRITING BY AMERICAN NEGROES

DAVID LITTLEJOHN

GROSSMAN PUBLISHERS
NEW YORK 1966

Copyright © 1966 by David Littlejohn

Published simultaneously in Canada by Fitzhenry and Whiteside

Library of Congress Catalog Card Number: 66–19523

MANUFACTURED IN THE UNITED STATES OF AMERICA

FIRST PRINTING

All the care possible has been taken to obtain permission from the copyright owners to reprint articles and selections protected by copyright; any errors or omissions are unintentional and will be rectified in any future printings upon notification to the author, who wishes to express his gratitude for permission to reprint material from the following sources:

The Beacon Press for quotations from:
  Notes of a Native Son by James Baldwin.

The Dial Press, Inc., for quotations from:
  The Fire Next Time © 1962, 1963 by James Baldwin.
  Nobody Knows My Name © 1954, 1956, 1958, 1959, 1960, 1961 by James Baldwin.
  Another Country © 1962 by James Baldwin.

Prof. Owen Dodson for a passage from his story "Come Home Early, Chile."

Harper & Row, Publishers for:
  Fragment of verse from "To John Keats, Poet at Spring Time" (p. 42), "Fruit of the Flower" (p. 14), and "Heritage" (p. 26) from *On These I Stand* by Countee Cullen. Copyright 1925 by Harper & Brothers; renewed 1953 by Ida M. Cullen.
  Excerpt from *Maud Martha* by Gwendolyn Brooks. Harper & Brothers, 1953.
  Poem "XV" ("Men of careful Turns . . .") from *Selected Poems* by Gwendolyn Brooks. Copyright 1945, 1949 by Gwendolyn Brooks Blakely.

Robert Hayden and October House for a quotation from the poem "Middle Passage."

Indiana University Press for a quotation from the poem "And the Old Women Gathered" by Mari Evans, from *New Negro Poets: U.S.A.*, edited by Langston Hughes.

FOR *SHEILA*

CONTENTS

CONTENTS

BLACK
ON
WHITE

I
INTRODUCTION

THE PAINS

It may one day be different, but a white American today will find it an exhausting and depressing enterprise to immerse himself for long in the recent literature of the American Negro—for a number of reasons. Much of the writing, like much of the writing of any race, is simply poor, the product of small minds that happen to be Negro. But aesthetic pain is a minor pain; more dispiriting is the simple experience of dwelling in the dull dark prison yard that is so often the Negro writer's world. A white reader is saddened, then burdened, then numbed by the deadly sameness, the bleak wooden round of ugly emotions and ugly situations; the same small frustrated dreams, the same issues and charges and formulas and events repeated over and over, in book after book. Economic oppression, dehumanization, ignominious role playing, the constant dealings with the very bottom of the human heap—the responding spirit is dulled, finally, bored by the iteration of hopelessness, the sordid limitation of the soul in the tight closet of the black imagination.

Not all of the poems and plays and novels of the American Negro, of course, are miserably bleak—only most of them; but even the few positive works still convey heavily to a white reader the sense of the "prison," of the debasing life sentence that being a Negro can

3

mean in America. Taken all together, the works of recent American Negro authors evoke a closed, colorless, nonexistensive world that the most despairing white existentialist will never know.

There is also a moral exhaustion involved in reading these works, which is more painful than even stylistic abrasion or imaginative claustrophobia. The occasion and the substance of most Negro writing in America is still the undeclared race war in which all Americans are, by definition, involved. This writing often becomes a weapon in the race war, and from the point of view of white readers, an enemy weapon. Some of it is meant to give pain, to disconcert and unbalance. Now, a great deal of literature will give pain, will disconcert and unbalance—momentarily. But as the product of integrated imaginations, more or less at peace, it will provide the reader with a means of digesting the pain, of attaining a new and better balance. "The excellence of every art is its intensity, capable of making all disagreeables evaporate . . ." The pain in most Negro literature of the American race war, however, remains solid and undigestable. It juts up, it rankles, it rubs raw like an ulcer. As it is meant to.

Sometimes the design is quite conscious: writing is one way of getting back at the enemy. The Negro's satisfaction will be doubled, of course, if his foolish white reader can be made to pay for and to praise the materials of his own discomfort. Such a conscious intent to give pain is clearly present, for example, in the plays of LeRoi Jones, the colored writer in America most notoriously possessed by the race-war concept of literature. Richard Wright's fiction, from the very start, was designed not simply to describe violence, to represent it,

4

but to be an act of violence itself. Even James Baldwin, who tries so hard to stay balanced and upright, will at times leap into the field of battle and flail away with belligerent unreason.

> White Americans seem to feel that happy songs are *happy* and sad songs are *sad*, and that, God help us, is exactly the way most white Americans sing them—sounding, in both cases, so helplessly, defensively fatuous that one dare not speculate on the temperature of the deep freeze from which issue their brave and sexless little voices.
>
> (James Baldwin, *The Fire Next Time*)

Rufus Scott and his sister Ida talk like this often in *Another Country*. Surely the insult, the anti-white affront is not entirely an accident of the creative unconscious.

Such works are designed, with more or less open intent (more in the case of Jones, less in the cases of Wright and Baldwin), to assert the moral superiority of the oppressed, and to force the unoppressed to grovel in guilt and fear. The "white liberal" reader—the term is one of scorn in some Negro circles—if he is not conscious of active guilt, is at least conscious of his exemption from suffering, which can be made to seem every bit as shameful. If he is not an oppressor, he is still one of the unfairly unoppressed.

From his supposedly comfortable position, the white reader, however pure of heart, may find it absurdly difficult to ward off the blow, to say no to the Joneses and Baldwins. He is forced, in a marvelous turnabout of traditional roles, to assume ridiculous poses and postures. Typically (as in Irving Howe's "Black Boys and Native Sons") he relinquishes moral and critical clarity in the

5

anxious effort to jump on some pro-Negro bandwagon he has made. He may even (as in Norman Mailer's "The White Negro") plead that he is really, at heart, a Negro himself. The contemplation of such moral contortions must provide Negro observers with at least partial revenge.

But even those Negro writers who are driven by no great urge to wound or revenge—and such generosity is not often to be expected—can produce in white readers the same uneasiness, even pain. Why is this?

In the first place, many of the works, especially the lesser novels of the Richard Wright tradition, depend very considerably on sadism or brutality. Unquestionably sadism and brutality form, continue to form, thanks to the American Negro's fellow citizens, a major aspect of his heritage. Such episodes will, probably should, be continually redramatized. But readers of all races will continue to respond with the imaginative equivalent of nausea.

Behind the sadism and brutality, secondly, are the sadists and brutes, the legions of bitches and boors, of near subhuman moral monsters who throng the pages of Negro writing. Detached from its specific national/racial setting, the literature of American Negroes may be read as one giant case against man at his worst. Even the white reader philosophic enough not to identify himself in guilt with these disgusting (white) human specimens, not to read them as personal indictments, will see in the genuineness of their portraits a dispiriting, Swiftian reminder that man, at his low point, is incredibly vicious and foul. It is not a pleasant reminder, and Negro literature hammers it in.

Thirdly, there is the pain of comparative class con-

6

sciousness excited in sensitive, leisured readers by the
experience of proletarian literature—and American Negroes, certainly, compose this country's proletariat, "the
lowest social or economic class of a community" in
Webster's definition. A leisured white reader will feel
not only the existential comfort of being white, but
also the relative comfort of being sufficiently educated,
wealthy, and at ease to be sitting reading a book about
the suffering poor. The contrast between his position
and theirs induces reflection so depressing, so empty,
and so generally fruitless that it may well be called pain.

Fourthly, there will always be a strain in the attempt
to respond to works that engage deep and bewildering
emotions. Just what the emotions are in this case, the
dark passions beneath the race war, is still something
of a mystery, hedged round with a lot of preconscious
taboos. The whole idea of race, of blood, has something
about it primevally disturbing. The mythic force of
color, of Blackness and Whiteness, resonates deep in
the American spirit. Inwrought here too, somewhere,
is the Western myth of Africa, of the awesome Heart
of Darkness, kept constantly alive to the sensitive and
superstitious imaginations of white Americans by the
skins and facial structures of their Negro neighbors.
And beneath it all run the underground currents of sex
—sexual envy, sexual fear, sexual desire: the root, no
doubt, of America's racial dilemma.

> . . . there is probably no greater (or more mis-
> leading) body of sexual myths in the world today
> than those which have proliferated around the fig-
> ure of the American Negro. This means that he is
> penalized for the guilty imagination of the white

people who invest him with their hates and long-
ings, and is the principal target of their sexual
paranoia.

(James Baldwin, *Nobody Knows My Name*)

The imaginative literature of American Negroes stirs
up all these radical emotions, brings the psychic foun-
dations of race hatred very close to conscious surface.
It is no wonder that even less belligerent examples can
be profoundly disturbing.

Fifthly, for a number of reasons—the lives Negro
writers have led, their motivations for writing, the pressures on them to be "race men"—the substantial content of Negro writing often seems to be nothing more
than a catalogue of white oppression. Richard Wright's
Black Boy (1945), and the communist lawyer's speech
in his *Native Son* (1940) fixed the pattern; Wright's
own later novels, and those of Chester Himes, Julian
Mayfield, Carl Offord, James O. Killens, W. G. Smith,
and others repeat the design. Poems like Margaret
Walker's "For My People," Robert Hayden's "Middle
Passage," Wright's "Between the World and Me" continue the technique—the unrolling of the white man's
abuse of the Negro in America, from the inhuman
slave ships and plantations of ante-bellum days through
the lynchings and beatings and brutalization and the
stunting economic imprisonment of yesterday and today. Negro literature often appears to be nothing more
than a recital of this litany of abuse. And though the
white reader may never before have felt any particular
race kinship with other whites, though he may himself
be the most benevolent of humanists, in the face of this

harrowing creative evidence he will frequently allow the responsibility for all white cruelty to Negroes to devolve, somehow, on himself.

Why this assumption of guilt? Why should beneficent, intelligent white readers take to themselves (or pretend to take to themselves) moral responsibility for all the bestial Southern peasants and Chicago policemen who happen to share their color? For the same reason, perhaps, that Negro readers felt ashamed of black Bigger Thomas, the immoralist hero of Wright's *Native Son*. A race war (even a literary race war), like any other war, intensifies one's sense of identification with the Side, the Team. The literature of the race war polarizes Americans; it forces them to take sides they would rarely take in life.

Moreover, many of the black heroes of these books assert the shared responsibility of all white men. They draw no distinction between the just and the unjust; they, the poor characters (or their creators), blame or hate *all* white men.

> Though thou hast sworn the sin is theirs alone,
> Their guilt is no whit greater than thy own.
> > (George Allen, "Pilate in Modern
> > America," in *Negro Caravan*)

Or as Ida Scott puts it in Baldwin's *Another Country*, "All you white bastards are the same."

This assertion may be detailed and absolute, like that of Bigger Thomas' lawyer or Baldwin's (Negro) self-projections. Or it may simply take the form of figures of speech, quiet and assured: Ofay, The Man, Mr. White Man, Mister Charlie, Whitefolks, the White

9

Devil, "White is Right." Or even the simple, damning question of a fictional Negro child: "Mama, what makes white folks so mean?"

This polarization, with the implicit assumption of all the suffering by one side and all the guilt by the other, is enforced by the frequent and usually unnoticed use of We-They rhetoric in Negro writing, a usage that presumes the myth and fosters the fact of racial war: of We versus They. James Baldwin (who has, or once had, the power to become an American National Conscience) depends to an unhappy degree on this device. He mixes the two pronouns with flagrant imprecision, adopting all positions to himself by turns, until even the emotional truth of his rhetoric is corrupted. In any case, the dogmatic use by Negro writers of the warring-camp pronouns helps to enforce in white readers the disturbingly irrational sensation that their hands are on every whip and every torch. (The habit is not confined to Negroes: Police Chief Parker of Los Angeles declared, when victory over the 1965 Watts rioters seemed to be near, "We're on the top now and they're on the bottom.")

A number of Negro authors—Richard Wright is again the classic case, but Chester Himes, LeRoi Jones, and others have followed—intensify the white reader's moral dilemma by positing "immoralist" black heroes, all but defying the white reader to object. This may be a simple act of war, designed to entrap the white reader, to make him squirm; it may be intended to demonstrate the brutalizing effect of oppression (as in *Native Son*); it may simply be a nonracial assertion of Immoralism. But whatever their purpose, such creations thwart the white reader's need to make moral

10

discriminations in fiction. There is no doubt of the "Power of Blackness" to intimidate the judge and to blunt the judgment. This is not to say that all white Americans may not, in some metaphysical way, be responsible for the plight of all Negro Americans—as all Germans, in some people's thinking, are responsible for the Jewish pogroms, or all sinners responsible for the death of Christ. Such speculations, however, I find singularly impractical. They are unlikely ever to ease the discomforts of either Negro or white. Let us confine ourselves, so far as possible, to more useful ground.

THE ESCAPES

Several responses to these discomforts are possible, other than abject groveling, or slapping a book closed, stomping out of the theater.

The wounded white reader/auditor may choose to regard such books and plays as documentary accounts, and then dismiss them as inaccurate (the Southern philistine's answer to Faulkner). People aren't really like that, he can prove; things aren't that bad. Or he may claim that writers are by nature extremists; that they are abnormal, sick, shrill, paranoiac, hypersensitive, atypical; and Negro writers especially. Their attacks, therefore, may be dismissed or discounted. Lynchings are now more common in fiction than they are in fact; not one Negro in ten thousand suffers the spiritual anguish of James Baldwin; the only Negroes who write are those who hate exceptionally.

He may go further and elude the intended lash by the armor of pride, by moral smugness: how *good* of me to be reading these ranting Negro works!

11

Americans, unhappily, have the most remarkable ability to alchemize all bitter truths into an innocuous but piquant confection and to transform their moral contradictions, or public discussion of such contradictions, into a proud decoration . . . The "protest" novel, so far from being disturbing, is an accepted and comforting aspect of the American scene . . . we receive a very definite thrill of virtue from the fact that we are reading such a book at all.

(James Baldwin, *Notes of a Native Son*)

The wounded white reader may even try to reduce out the color content, and claim that these are simply the histories of any oppressed minority, regardless of race. (And then confront that accusation as he will.)

Even the painful, raceless reminder of the vileness of man may be used by the sophistical reader to elude the *intended*, the less philosophical pain of racist antagonism; to pretend away the specific, the current, the very American nastiness of race-war writing. One can bemoan, on his bald mountaintop, the human debasement symbolized by an Alabama lynch mob, forgetting that, to a Negro, the mob is not only symbolic.

Such attempts to deflect the pain of Negro writing are like the evasion-interpretations, the "explainings-away" of Book IV of *Gulliver's Travels*. Horses really aren't Houyhnhnms, you know; people really aren't Yahoos. Gulliver has obviously gone mad; Swift was psychotically misanthropic, and so on.

The last, the most sophisticated escape, in such cases, is through "literary" judgment: It's poorly done. Amen. End of problem. One tends to fall back on this last evasion (if it is an evasion) quite frequently in the case of the more militant Negro literature: It isn't literature. Propaganda with a plot (or in rhyme, or in acts). Unconvincing; lifeless; unearned; unfelt; uncrafted. Such criticisms *are* often only illicit self-defenses against pain; a reader slips on the rubber gloves of criticism to avoid the sting. But has he, the white reader, then, no right to make literary judgments—in wartime, as it were? Many of these critiques, interior or in print, are of the nature of moral evasions; but many of the wounds being evaded are illicit and unfair. Is the white reader simply to sit there, turning pages and squirming?

Before answering this question of critical evaluation, let us consider first *why* a white reader might want to bother with all this painful reading in the first place; and then how he ought to treat it.

THE REASONS

One reason white audiences may devote themselves to Negro literature is the customary dim sense of obligation concerning racial affairs. Another, probably more common, is the popular vogue at present (though nothing like the "Harlem Renaissance" craze of the twenties) for several authors—James Baldwin and LeRoi Jones in particular.

A more honorable reason for interesting oneself in Negro writing, if one is white, is the constant, nagging white American's urge to know "what Negroes are like." The white American of good will is disturbed by his culpable ignorance. He is likely never, unfortunately, to have met a Negro on intimate terms; or, if he has, to have felt capable, for all his good intentions, of penetrating beyond the forbidding brownish integument.

"I could not help wondering," James Baldwin wrote of a white man, "if he had ever really *looked* at a Negro and wondered about the life, the aspirations, the universal humanity hidden behind the dark skin." Many, of course, have not; but many have, and have turned away bewildered. A white clergyman, last year, trying to conciliate between policemen and demonstrators in Washington, D.C., asked a young Negro why he was lying down in the middle of the street. "Because I'm black. You wouldn't understand." In a sense, half the race war will be over the day white Americans come truly to "know" Negroes as human beings, to understand the experience of being a Negro. William Faulkner, who of all people might at least have had an idea, "could not imagine himself a Negro for two minutes."

At present, when an American white man tries to imagine himself black, the resultant sensation is likely to be a shudder of gratitude that he is not, the whole idea is so compact with pity and fear. All the white man knows is the outside reactions he would encounter if he *were* colored, because these reactions have been his own: curiosity, the patronizing stare, the glazed sad eyes; he would be treated always, he knows, for better or worse, as the exception, be looked at like a pair of mysterious hard-boiled eggs in a mahogany mask. What he does *not* know are the inner resources he might muster—he would still be human, after all—to meet such ignorance. He does not know the quality of the life within, or the life outside when no white men are present. Ralph Ellison (in *Shadow and Act*, 1965) has

14

tried very hard to convince white Americans that Negroes *do* lead rich, varied, complicated lives; that the worlds Negroes make and find, inside and out, are not just the bleak torture chambers sympathetic white men have imagined, driven by Richard Wright and their prickly consciences.

It is this ignorance, this lamentable failure of imagination that the reading of Negro literature can help to correct. The creative writing of American Negroes *can* begin to lead outsiders to an understanding of "what Negroes are like." It will never make a Negro of one born white. However vivid the experience of reading, a white reader will always retreat into his profitable whiteness when the reading is done. Still, the good book, the powerful poem *will* change the reader somehow; he will carry away in himself some portion of Negro experience, now made a part of his own.

And the truths will not be simply learned, as from interviews or sociological texts, but coexperienced, borne "alive into the heart with passion." Here is reason enough for reading this disturbing collection. If it turns out as well to be good, if purely literary, extraracial benefits accrue in the meantime, of course so much the better.

DISCRIMINATIONS

This brings us back, though, to the question of whether there is any useful distinction to be made between better and worse. As much can be learned, one might claim, from the failures of Negro art, the fixations, the authorial neuroses, as from the fully achieved creations of integrated minds. By the author's standards, moreover, it may well be the degree of unalleviated pain caused that matters, the dynamic, unidirectional intensity of the reader's reaction: not some high and harmonious reconstruction of the spirit, or whatever the effect of fine art is taken to be. These books may be meant as high explosives, racial textbooks, and not *objets d'art*. Some few, in addition, may be written specifically for other Negroes.

The pain, the moral oppression—the "war" element —is too evidently a fact of the reading to be ignored. It severely conditions any white critical response, it blocks most attempts at imaginative participation. Robert Bone, in *The Negro Novel in America* (1958, revised 1965), attempted to confine his discussion to "formal" literary criticism, to structure, symbolic patterns, prose style, and the like. The result was somehow fidgety, uncomfortably precious. Some very large thing seemed to be missing.

It is wrong to try to ignore or deny the pain caused by strong protest literature. But no one white reader can tell another that (or how) he should suffer. Literary criticism is subjective enough, without becoming confessional. Let us grant that the white American reader ought to let himself be tested by these works, by the writings of people men of his color have tormented. But let us also grant that this testing is very much a private affair. The only conclusions he can draw from the test will apply to his own attitudes and behavior; they cannot be extended into monitions or standards or valuations for anyone else. Reading for self-examination and reading for objective evaluation are two different undertakings: not everything that can

16

be said about a work should always be said out loud.

There may even be an absolute difference, for critical purposes, between dynamic or "protest" literature—the book as missile—and literature that is self-contained and harmonious, between literature that hates and literature that loves, between *The Dutchman*, say, and *Go Tell It on the Mountain*. If this is the case, then quite different sets of standards will apply to the two, and it would be idiotic to ask a work of one sort to be a work of the other. Henry James should not be asked to review Dostoevsky, nor a Jamesian to review Jean Genet. As it turns out, since very few Negro works are pure anything, pure protest or pure "art," this distinction is simply another way of asserting that the *dynamic* element, the element of pain, should not be ignored—even by the professional white critic. He, too, after hours, is a moral agent.

But aesthetic judgment, *total* judgment of American Negro literature, even without this distinction, is not just an irrelevant luxury to be indulged in, "after the war is over." Even on our standard of information, the education of the white imagination to the truths of Negro experience, it is the achieved, the balanced, the self-contained works that will embrace the widest domains of truth. Not all teaching is done by facts—even "true" facts. The protest novels, the pain-causing works can tell only part of the story. The greater art is to contain, to hold together more, the suffering *and* the joy, the hate and the love. This is the fine point of Ralph Ellison's answer to Irving Howe, who insisted (in "Black Boys and Native Sons") that *all* Negro writers should be producing hate novels in the Richard Wright tradition.

. . . Evidently Howe feels that unrelieved suffering is the only "real" Negro experience, and that the true Negro writer must be ferocious. But there is also an American Negro tradition which teaches one to deflect racial provocation and to master and contain pain. . . . even as life toughens the Negro, even as it brutalizes him, sensitizes him, dulls him, goads him to anger, moves him to irony, sometimes fracturing and sometimes affirming his hopes; even as it shapes his attitudes towards family, sex, love, religion; even as it modulates his humor, tempers his joy—it *conditions* him to deal with his life and with himself.

(Ralph Ellison, *Shadow and Act*)

Wright's novels, and others like them, can tell the reader about their authors, show him something of the shape the war myth can take in Negro imaginations. But, as Ralph Ellison points out (with all respect), Richard Wright is, among Negroes, an extraordinary freak. *His* Negro world exists only in his books and in his angry unconscious mind. It is, unlike the "real" Negro world, entirely devoid of tenderness, love, communality, loyalty, music, religious faith and hope, all of the solace and all of the joy. It is still *true*, since it is true for Wright, and full of salutary pain; but its educational value is negative or small. One can, with care, learn something of "what it is like to be a Negro" from the single-minded activist; but he can learn far, far more from calmer, more careful writers who try harder to tell the whole truth. It is for this reason that the artists and works of art among Negro letters are especially to be treasured by white readers—the hum-

18

bler, the more careful: Langston Hughes, Ann Petry, Gwendolyn Brooks, the James Baldwin of *Go Tell It on the Mountain*. Incorporated into Ellison's *Invisible Man* is more of what matters of the Negro's experience of America than in a dozen burning novels of protest—if we only knew how to find it, if we only had the patience and the skill to extract it.

Even by the standard of "salutary pain," the works of true art have a case. We should distinguish between varieties of mental anguish—some are more useful than others.

The greatest discomfort involved in reading the works of the enemy (and also the most valuable) was not included in my catalogue of pains at the start of this essay. It is not aesthetic distaste, or imaginative claustrophobia, or the revulsion from horror, or the view of human depravity, or the arousal of uncomfortable passions. It is not even the moral intimidation—exacerbated class consciousness, impotence in the face of insult, the heavy weight of shared white guilt, the paralysis of one's moral sensibility. The greatest, the most salutary discomfort may rather be the proper *resisting* of all these, insofar as they ought to be resisted. A proper reading, an honest evaluation, will be the hardest task of all—and the most liberating. It may be superhumanly difficult for a Negro writer to keep straight his moral bearings in the face of his white tormentor, but the "white tormentor," as reader, has his obligations too. It is all too morally easy to grovel, to cringe beneath the lash. Not all the history of racial oppression in America should be allowed to paralyze the moral sensibility, the critical faculty, the ability even of white men to "discriminate," or the war has

indeed been lost. To read with a sharp, Gidean conscience ever awake, monitoring, regulating, correcting;
to resist the unfair imposition, the bullying intimidation; but to acknowledge, too, to accept and heed the
insults that are deserved: this is the way to read the
literature of war.

And it is the better works, one finds, that require the
most total self-examinations, the most radical self-sur-
gery.

> Heavenly Hurt, it gives us—
> We can find no scar,
> But internal difference,
> Where the Meanings are.

I found the sheer effort of discrimination involved, for
example, in reading James Baldwin's two collections
of essays so internally exhausting, the expense of spirit
in honest evaluation so arduous and so demanding, that
it proved impossible to read more than a few essays a
day. (And *not*, necessarily, because Baldwin is always
telling the truth; no one tells half-truths so eloquently.)
It is hard to keep one's wits about one while being
beaten—especially if one envies the flagellator's style.
The real pain of reading the Negro literature of the race
war is as oppressive as it is beneficial. If a new truth
does not really hurt—not "literarily," but really—it is
probably no truth.

We have considered what the experience might be
of a white reader confronting the American Negro in
his literature: why he might do it, how he should do it.
It is time to see what this literature is.

20

II
BEFORE *NATIVE SON:*
THE DARK AGES

I originally intended to concentrate this discussion on
the writings of American Negroes since 1940, the publication date of Richard Wright's *Native Son.* It is then
that serious American Negro literature begins, literature that need not be qualified or justified or apologized
for. With the possible exception of Langston Hughes,
I would feel compelled to include the work of no Negro
writer before 1940 in a fair critical survey of American
literature. "Major" American Negro writing is a very
recent phenomenon.

Moreover, as I have noted, there is a correspondence
between literary and educational value. Much can be
learned of the Negro's experience in America from the
poems and novels of his earlier generations. But rarely
does the effective relevance of such works extend into
our own time. The honky-tonk, jazz-baby Harlem of the
Negro novels of the twenties, for example, could hardly
be more pathetically irrelevant to the Harlem of today.
And this same judgment could be made of most of these
writings, now about as pertinent as nineteenth-century
minstrel shows. A musty datedness, the sickly nostalgic
scent of the ardently unfashionable, lingers about almost all this early work. Few Negro literary imaginations before Richard Wright's (and even his work, as
we shall see, has mildewed a bit) were capacious
enough, free enough to see beyond their own decade.
Their works, which often bore the original disfigure-

ment of an adolescent racial anxiety, an unskilled and excessive introspection, have shriveled into "period pieces", with all the sad, small provincialisms of their birthdate clearly evident.

But some sense of source and context and continuity may be useful. So before turning to the literature of the last twenty-five years, I shall note, in this chapter and the next, some of the earlier Negro works that nod above the lot; and suggest the varying impressions they give of Negro experience in America before the present generation, their varying kinds of irrelevance.

Negroes in America have been writing and publishing as long as white masters, slave owners and publishers, have allowed them to do so. The anthologies for use in Negro schools usually begin with Phillis Wheatley, a Massachusetts slave girl whose pious poems were printed in 1773. From Phillis Wheatley to the Harlem Renaissance of the 1920's, few colored Americans had the training or the leisure to write, and their scattered efforts were at best mediocre. These efforts took the form, most often, of either Old Black Joe dialect tales or poorer imitations of poor white models: genteel fictions, village librarian's verse.

The verse need not detain us long. It is preserved today exclusively in "race" anthologies, and none of it would be in print if its authors were not Negroes. The very earliest, the ante-bellum verse, can only afford a perverse anthropological interest ("Imagine—a Negro slave writing poems!"); "undistinguished" is too kind a word. Most of the work of the next phase, the Gilded Age (1865-1920), recalls the jingling, simple, sentimental stuff one used to memorize in school: homely ideas forced out of shape to make them fit the verse, "poems" only insofar as they rhyme. The corny dialect pieces, the melancholy, watery-Tennysonian stanzas of these Negro versemakers are no worse than the efforts of most of their white American contemporaries; but this is not saying very much. They are decent, dated, well-intended album pieces for the most part, a warm balm to good small souls, and an inspiration to race-proud Negroes. Some few of the poets (or poetesses: Georgia Douglass Johnson, Angelina Grimke, Anne Spencer) managed to avoid the grosser faults, the cruder poetic diction, to trip their meters and sketch their little pictures with some skill. They admired their Browning, they wrote agreeable recital numbers, they loved the sonnet form; and one is loath to criticize them heavily. But there is no reason for grownups to read them, unless they are writing books on Negro poetry.

Two poets of the pre-Renaissance period stand slightly apart—Paul Dunbar and James Weldon Johnson—if only for their celebrity. Dunbar is probably still the best-known Negro poet among Negroes. For many years he was a race hero in the company of Joe Louis and Booker T. Washington, and his disfavor (like theirs) among the intelligentsia may take a while to spread to the lower orders. He was a successful magazine poet of the turn of the century (he died at thirty-four), sponsored by William Dean Howells; a master sentimentalist who wrung the heart of a simpler America. Today, reading his collected poems—three hundred pages of Golden Book moralism, purple poesy, and dialect pastorals in the James Whitcomb Riley vein, of hometown nostalgia and barbershop wisdom ("Keep a-Pluggin' Away")—is like eating jars of peanut butter. He was lionized for his "plantation nigger" narratives ("When de Co'n Pone's Hot," "When Malindy Sings"), which even uncritical Negroes might find hard to take today. Only two or three poems—"We Wear the Mask," "I Know What the Caged Bird Feels"—appear to hide genuine, adult, and still honorable emotions.

James Weldon Johnson (1871-1938), a contemporary of Dunbar's, outlived him to become one of the most distinguished Negro Americans of his time: a lyricist for Broadway shows, U.S. Consul in Venezuela and Nicaragua, a teacher, attorney, novelist, poet, editor, professor, and executive secretary of the NAACP. His autobiography, *Along This Way*, is one of the more dependable and readable of Negro leaders' autobiographies. His noteworthy "serious" poems are black propaganda pieces in nineteenth-century rhetoric, on the "This Land Is Our Land" theme; they include, in "Brothers" (1917), what may be the first outspoken dramatization of a lynching in verse.

His claim to a degree of poetic celebrity, however, rests on *God's Trombones* and "St. Peter Relates an Incident," both written well after the end of the period in question, though still obviously the work of an older writer. The former, a collection of seven imitations of Negro sermons, once appeared striking and original; but so many examples of the colored preacher's sermon have appeared since (Faulkner's, Ellison's, Baldwin's, Ossie Davis', etc.), examples more compulsive, more stirring and effective, that Johnson's versions may read today like tame, overcivilized outlines, without the real spirit, the crescendo rhythms, the extraordinary imagery one associates with the genre. Although "The

Creation" is the best known, "Judgment Day" strikes me as the best, the most rhapsodic and rolling. Certain sequences of others are effective—the Flood in "Noah Built an Ark," Pharoah's Army in "Let My People Go," the nailing on the cross in "The Crucifixion"—

> Jesus, my lamb-like Jesus,
> Shivering as the nails go through his hands;
> Jesus, my lamb-like Jesus,
> Shivering as the nails go through his feet.
> Jesus, my darling Jesus,
> Groaning as the Roman spear plunged in his
> side;
> Jesus, my darling Jesus,
> Groaning as the blood came spurting from
> his wound.
> Oh, look how they done my Jesus.

But the collection as a whole still seems slightly anthropological-condescending, a book of imitations far less potent than their originals.

There are no important novels by American Negroes written before 1923. Paul Dunbar wrote a number of his harmless "plantation nigger" folk stories in a manner less aggressively sentimental than that of his poems, stories told half in dialect, half in an orotund, authorial-declamatory voice. Two or three make what is, for Dunbar, strong anti-slavery or anti-lynching protests; but they are outbalanced by a far greater number of reactionary pieces or worse, depicting plantation darkies as jolly children all, whose best friend—even after Emancipation—was always Ol' White Massa.

J. W. Johnson's *The Autobiography of an Ex-Colored Man* (1912) is more a social phenomenon than a novel, and its notoriety—some of which has endured —is the combined product of its once-daring title, its anonymous publication (which led readers to presume it factual for fifteen years), and the novelty of its "outspoken" message to 1912 America. It reveals itself today as an utterly artless, unstructured, unselective sequence of Negro-life episodes, written in a style as flat and directionless as the floor of an enormous room. The climactic episodes, moreover—the hero's high life in Bohemian New York as a ragtime pianist, his European tour with a millionaire patron—betray only adolescent fantasies beneath the dull surface of prose. More interesting is what Johnson reveals, of America and himself, between the lines of plot. His essayette digressions, for example, offer a fair view of the antediluvian race relations in America during this period, albeit a view peculiarly fogged by his own prejudices: W. E. B. DuBois is a far more dependable authority. The prejudices themselves, though, the self-revelation, may have for some white readers still a strangely pathetic appeal. He—the "hero," if not Johnson—is a pure example of the self-styled "better class of Negroes," a member of DuBois' "Talented Tenth," who hoped in these distant, deluded years to effect a liaison with "the better class of whites," and to detach himself utterly from the despised lower Negro classes.

> The unkempt appearance, the shambling slouching gait and loud talk and laughter of these people aroused in me a feeling of almost repulsion.
> . . . odd as it may sound, refined coloured peo-

ple get no more pleasure out of riding with offensive Negroes than anybody else would get. . . .

Happily, this class represents the black people
of the South far below their normal physical and
moral condition, but in its increase lies the possibility of grave dangers. . . .

I can imagine no more dissatisfied being than
an educated, cultured, and refined coloured man
in the United States.

Along with this class consciousness goes a dilettan-
tish championing of the popular Negro arts, reminis-
cent of the detached folklorist's interest one feels in
God's Trombones. His hero lists, in fact, the Uncle
Remus stories, the Jubilee songs, ragtime, and the cake-
walk as the four great cultural contributions of the
American Negro, and paragraphs of his prose are de-
voted to the latter two. *The Autobiography* is anything
but a "good" book; but, for all the naïveté, the snobbery, the fantasy, and the flatness, it does afford a
unique and perhaps useful portrait of a period and a
type.

Charles Chesnutt was a better writer than either
Dunbar or Johnson, although still very small beer. As
with the lesser lady poets, it would be ungracious and
inappropriate to press criticism too hard. He was, like
some later Negro writers—Walter White, Jean Toomer
—what is called a "voluntary" Negro; that is to say, a
Negro only by Southern legal definition, one who could,
on appearance, easily have led the life of a white man.
This may help to explain the detached, cool ease of his
narrative voice, the voice of an urbane white (or near-
white) Northern observer viewing the battered and de-

27

moralized post-bellum South. Like Dunbar, he wrote
out of the Plantation Tradition; but his new narrative
stance, both in person and in time, allows him to show
more clearly the truths of its decay. Images of decay, in
fact, of the weed-grown fields and arbors, of the listless
town squares, of the fallen shanties and the ruined man-
sions of the New South, set an appropriate stage for his
critique of the society. The attack is outspoken only in
The Marrow of Tradition (1901) and *The Colonel's
Dream* (1905), though even these are genteel melodramas first, strong criticism second; but the portraits of
Southern bigotry and brutality, in a particularly brutal
era, are firmly drawn. *The House Behind the Cedars*
(1900) comes closer to pure melodrama, on the popular
but tasteless theme of the fair mulatto girl whose "taint
of black blood" is at last revealed to her shame and
doom. One can see the appeal of this theme to the sensa-
tion-hungry white gentility; but the adoption of it by
Chesnutt strikes one as rather low, and perhaps reveals him as not altogether happy in his choice of a
racial adoption. Chesnutt's "conjure woman" (a kind
of witch doctor) stories are droll, professional entertain-
ments in the traditional American semi-supernatural,
tall-tale vein, each with its amusing moral twist. "Mars'
Jeem's Dream," for all its charm and corn—the story is
that of a white master who is "conjured" black for a few
days on his own plantation—is one of the more powerful
allegorical fantasies of race-war literature, comparable
to George Schuyler's *Black No More* of 1931. Chesnutt's novels and stories are distinctly professional,
minor works of the American Gilded Age, with all the
limitations of diction, technique, and moral horizon
that that implies. But he is never mean or stupid, and

affords at his best some agreeable hours' reading to those who can make allowances for sixty years.

The best-known Negro writings of the period are not poems or novels at all, but the classic autobiographies and testaments: Frederick Douglass' *Life and Times* (1845, rep. 1941), Booker T. Washington's *Up From Slavery* (1901), and W. E. B. DuBois' *The Souls of Black Folk* (1903); to which I would add the afore-mentioned, though less essential *Along This Way* (1933) of James Weldon Johnson, to bring the story some years further along. Except for DuBois' book, I would make no claim for any of these as "literature"; the Douglass and Johnson works are fat, detailed, episodic memoirs of the usual unliterary sort, important for the history they reveal and for their central perspective on the Negro story. And in sixty-five years, the reputation of *Up From Slavery* has plummeted from that of a work of near-Biblical inspiration and authority, to that of a textbook of all that was wrong in the Negro's past ef-forts, a despised handbook for Uncle Toms; a symbol, like Chamberlain's umbrella, of hateful appeasement.

Seen clearly, dispassionately, and in context, it is not quite either. It must be assessed, as must Booker T. him-self, his Tuskegee Institute, and the whole "Tuskegee Idea," as a total social force; and ultimately, in the moral realm, as one pole of the most celebrated controversy in American Negro history. This is no place to reenact the complex drama, as old and as fundamental as Antigone's argument with Creon. I refer the interested reader—the Washington-DuBois controversy is an issue constantly raised in subsequent Negro writing, and it would be well to know the facts—to Hugh Hawkins' excellent casebook of essays, *The Booker T. Washington Con-*

troversy (New York, 1962), and to the full works from which his selections are taken.

But a word, at least, on *Up From Slavery* as a book: there is honestly nothing I can say on its behalf as art, biography, moral exemplum, or an instance of humane and admirable thought. It was written as a weapon for philanthropy and prestige by a Puritan materialist of astonishing proportions (and astonishing skill), and it served his purpose. The book is dominated by several inter-involved beliefs: an absolute faith in laissez-faire capitalism and the business ethic (rich American businessmen are the best men in the world); an obsessive faith in hygiene and thrift and the dignity of manual labor; and an extraordinary, a limitless respect for Booker T. Washington—the book reads like a saint's life, written by the saint. Like Dickens' virtuous co-narratress in *Bleak House*, Washington is forced to the artless ruse of quoting everyone's praises of him, so as not to be praising himself directly all the time. He does no wrong, has no enemies, suffers hardships willingly, is universally beloved, and is, for it all (as he confesses), quite humble.

> Time and time again, as I have stood in the street in front of a building and have seen men and women passing in large numbers into the audience-room where I was to speak, I have felt ashamed that I should be the cause of people—as it seemed to me—wasting a valuable hour of time.

On his actual program, his advice to the Negro, his euphemistic, careful, even deceitful handling of white Southerners and men of power, I will not attempt to adjudicate, since all this is part of the great controversy.

30

"To criticize his methods," it has been claimed, "is to make the facile assumption that he had a choice. He did what was possible. . . ." All good men, we are reminded by one of his defenders, are "time-servers" of one sort or another.

He was, obviously, neither absolutely a fool nor absolutely a knave. It is best to regard him in the company of his friends Andrew Carnegie and Theodore Roosevelt, a man of the same vintage, stamp, and quality, and to assess him accordingly. He was a classic American anti-intellectual, who distrusted book learning, preferred newspapers to novels and Rotarians to professors, who wrote "Few things are more satisfactory to me than a high-grade Berkshire or Poland China pig." Any judgment of him or his work by a literary critic should probably be counterweighted with one by, say, an American business executive. A judgment between Washington and DuBois, in fact, in this anti-ideological day, may well reduce itself to one of those amoral, or supramoral preferences of "style" that Lionel Trilling so dislikes, like one's judgment between Kennedy and Johnson.

William Edward Burghardt DuBois has had the posthumous ill fortune to be memorialized since his death (in 1963, at ninety-five) for only the final and possibly least reputable stage of an epically long and various career. Only in his last years, in unhappy African exile, did he accept the relatively doctrinaire Marxist position the DuBois Clubs represent. Until then, he had insisted on maintaining an individualist, flexible, and frequently changing definition for his personal brand of social idealism. He had been, in his idealist's career, something of an internationalist, something of an anti-capitalist

31

from the start; but he was also an aristocratic humanist and libertarian. One only hopes that the DuBois Clubs' honest notoriety does not define the limits of his reputation. He was a very complex man.

His extraordinary career has been the subject of books: he is the sole Exemplary Man, the most important ethical spokesman among American Negroes before James Baldwin—whose manner, writing, and career begin in many ways to parallel DuBois', given the changing pressures of another half century's progress in the race war. I will not attempt to do him full justice here, but only discuss three of his published works: a collection of essays, a novel, and a poem; these, out of scores of titles—including a worthy trilogy of documentary novels he began at the age of ninety! It may be kept in mind, though, that I regard him as the most honest, perhaps the one honest and truly valuable Negro spokesman of his immature and alien time.

The Souls of Black Folk (1903), the collection of essays, probably deserves the name of "classic" that most commentators accord it. It is the only Negro work of its vintage that has worn so well, and it is likely to remain readable and pertinent—even eloquent, and necessary—for many decades to come. Its celebration in the early years of the century was, I grant, a testament to its historical importance, to its revolutionary outspokenness, and not to its "classical" durability. But DuBois' assertions still hold an uncanny prophetic relevance, perhaps even a causal relevance, to the events in the Civil Rights struggle since 1954. Moreover—a grim, lamentable reflection—many of his portraits, analyses, and accusations still apply. His discussion, for example (in the first and tenth chapters), of the Negro's racial psychol-

ogy in America—of the paralyzing tension of his double
identity, of his "morbid sense of personality," of the
elaborate stratagems of hypocrisy to which he is forced
—all this is as penetrating and contemporary as Richard
Wright's "The Ethics of Living Jim Crow" or the better essays of Baldwin's two collections.

But the important chapters of *The Souls of Black
Folk*—the fifth, eleventh, twelfth, thirteenth, and four-
teenth may be skipped—earn their classical status by
being, paradoxically, so distinctly of their time, by the
pressure of a temporal context one cannot help but feel.
1903—actually, the period from 1890 to 1910—probably represents the low point in the life story of the
American Negro, lower even than slavery. Much of my
admiration for DuBois is a response to his heroic ability
to be so honest, so eloquent, so hopeful and militant and
fair *at this time*, in 1903, when the state of the American race war had retrogressed so dismally that the average observer could have found cause for nothing but
despair. The racist South as we have come to recognize
it—"an armed camp for intimidating black folk"—and
all the grosser paraphernalia of racial repression, Northern and Southern (disfranchisement, peonage, crop-lien
"slavery," chain gangs, residential and educational segregation, Jim Crow in all his forms, the unequal justice
of courts and police)—all these took their start not in
slavery as such, not even in the Civil War and the bitter
Reconstruction, but in those frantic, doltish years before
the century's turn. And it was at this stage, after a dismal downhill progress of over thirty years; at a time
when the nation was virtually unanimous in its acceptance of the creed of innate Negro inferiority; at a time
when Booker Washington's pose of appeasement from

33

below was doubtless far, far more politic and wise; it
was at *this* moment that W. E. B. DuBois chose to tell
"the whole truth" to America.

He told, first, the truths of the past: in a corrective
historical essay on the Freedmen's Bureau of the Reconstruction; through his genuine sympathy for the dispossessed white masters and their sons; through his
peculiar understanding of the sufferings of a beaten
South; and in an exceptionally honest assessment of
American slavery:

> . . . not the worst slavery in the world, not a slav-
> ery that made all life unbearable, rather a slavery
> that had here and there something of kindliness,
> fidelity, and happiness—but withal slavery, which,
> so far as human aspiration and desert were con-
> cerned, classed the black man and the ox together.

He told, over and over (Chapters 4, 7, 8, 9), the
truths of the rural South of 1903, of the Southern social
system—peonage, rack-renting, the caste system, con-
vict leasing, white man's justice—in moving narrative
accounts of his journeys through the Black Belt. He
analyzed the systems and patterns of segregation and
prejudice, and described the internal effects of their brutalization: "the inner degradation, the hurt-hound feeling," which brought joy "at the sheerest and most negative decency." He admitted the ugly facts of Negro
crime and immorality, but then traced them to their
source. He took apart each paragraph of the rhetoric of
white supremacy, refuting a body of opinion almost
universally held. He even ventured the first outspoken
counter-argument to the white Southern cause of racial-
sexual purity: this in 1903.

The limitations of the book, like its peculiar nobilities, are in part the result of its time: if many of the issues remain alive, many others have died. In particular, the race war is now more an urban than a rural affair, and the Negro as adversary is considerably better armed. Beyond this, the book is dated and declassicized by DuBois' frequent leaps into purple prosing ("The Veil" is his image for the color line), by his proper Victorian sexual morality, and by his occasional invocations of a turgid, millenarian ideology. (The age of the book is felt most in Chapter 5, and in the last four pieces.) But a great deal endures.

Allowances for the era, and to some degree for the man, must be made more extensively and wholeheartedly in the case of DuBois' best novel, *The Quest for the Silver Fleece* (1911). Tolerance, patience of a most imaginative sort will be required of the sophisticated contemporary reader; but I think there are rewards. DuBois' fictional standards were not ours, and he indulged in the literary excesses of his era to a voluptuous degree. The limitations of the "fallen woman" morality, of a golden-hazy view of "love" do more harm to a novel than to a collection of essays. DuBois' faith in melodrama is touching, but its unrealism and excesses are likely to sap the strength of the book's better qualities today, and to alienate the kind reader. His two Negro heroes are sublimely heroic fantasy creatures who "move up," like Dickens' heroes, into society and wealth and great power—one of them determines the outcome of a presidential election. The villains, to balance, are diabolically villainous. The morally biased, cosmetic high color of both high life and low life; the crude caricatures of outsiders; the constant "high blood pressure"

35

effect of his frenziedly artificial events—one either winces at all this excess, or (a common effect of good melodrama) is ashamed of giving in.

Even this does not exhaust the list of faults: it is hardly a great book. But it is, I think, a good-hearted book, whose better qualities may still gleam through the thick hedge of its age and excesses. DuBois used this novel to dramatize his protests, to fight in fiction his battles against racial and economic injustice. He wrought a novel of economic epic pretensions and of genuinely mythic design. The patient reader of today will feel throughout the author's compassion, his indomitable moral strength. It *is* a hugely moral novel, a sturdy and masculine one; it is honorable and humane, and informed throughout with the sense and strength of W. E. B. DuBois.

A summing up of the values and limitations of the man himself, the most important Negro intellectual of the period, will provide a setting for my reference to his strongest poem. DuBois was, first and most importantly, the pioneer of the struggle for full civil rights, a battle he waged under primitive conditions for over thirty years. He defined, secondly, as exactly and fully as he knew how, a new situation in American culture, and tried through his definitions and his active work to prevent its growing worse—though never at the price of unwholesome compromise. He described to white America with sympathy and poise, thirdly, the life style and economic fact of Negro America, deflating much of the popular racial mythology. And he wrote, fourthly, in a style of distinction, exactness, and vigor.

A first limitation might be the qualification of this last virtue: the Carlylean hyperbole, the incantatory and overstylized excess of his more excited prose moments. Secondly, one may fault his belated Victorianism: his relish for the melodramatic, his preference for an art of genteel uplift, his restrictive and sentimental sexual ethic. Thirdly, he was, like James Weldon Johnson, something of a snob. Fourthly, when not responding directly or instinctually to a situation, he could tumble into great messes of ideological confusion: his career was a long chain of bizarre social visions. And fifthly—the obverse of his cosmopolitan elitism—he revealed himself often as a *Negro* racist, full of black-Zionist assertions about "Negro blood" and exclusivity. In this, he is spiritual grandfather to the black absolutists of our era, Richard Wright, James Baldwin, LeRoi Jones. Like Baldwin, he often assumed the messianic role of All-Negro, declaiming for The Race in the first person plural. Like Wright, he could delude himself with the specter of the active solidarity of all the "colored" races of the world, armed against the whites. Like Baldwin and Wright, he could fall into the moral trap of reserving all goodness, all honor to the side of the oppressed. ("We are the only artists in America.") And like all three, he could find momentary spiritual release in hate, in the wild imaginative sport of flogging the whites:

A city lay in travail, God our Lord, and from her loins sprang twin Murder and Black Hate. Red was the midnight; clang, crack and cry of death and fury filled the air and trembled underneath the stars when church spires pointed silently to Thee. And all this was to sate the greed of greedy men who hide behind the veil of vengeance!
Bend us Thine ear, O Lord! . . .

Doth not this justice of hell stink in Thy nostrils,
O God? How long shall the mounting flood of in-
nocent blood roar in Thine ears and pound in our
hearts for vengeance? Pile the pale frenzy of blood-
crazed brutes who do such deeds high on Thine
altar, Jehovah Jireh, and burn it in hell forever and
forever!

*Forgive us, Good Lord; we know not what we
say!*

Bewildered we are, and passion-tost, mad with
the madness of a mobbed and mocked and mur-
dered people; straining at the armposts of Thy
Throne, we raise our shackled hands and charge
Thee, God, by the bones of our stolen fathers, by
the tears of our dead mothers, by the very blood of
Thy crucified Christ: *What meaneth this?* Tell us
the Plan; give us the Sign!

Keep not Thou silence, O God!

Sit no longer blind, Lord God, deaf to our prayer
and dumb to our dumb suffering. Surely, Thou too
art not white, O Lord, a pale, bloodless, heartless
thing?

Ah! Christ of all the Pities!

("A Litany at Atlanta," 1906)

We should recognize the tone as contemporary, if not
the diction. The poem was occasioned by the Atlanta
Race Riot of 1906, and should be enough to certify the
relevance of this man to our time, to our stage of the
race war, for all his limitations. One has only to imagine
him born, with the same spirit and the same talents,
perhaps fifty years later.

III
BEFORE *NATIVE SON:*
THE RENAISSANCE AND AFTER

In retrospect, the Harlem Renaissance of 1923 to 1933 seems far less important a literary event than it did to some observers at the time. There is no question of its importance as a progressive movement, both real and symbolic, in American Negro culture. The question is rather that of its substantial worth in any other context, or its relevance to subsequent generations.

It was, in part, one more fad of the faddish twenties —something modish and insubstantial, and perhaps even a little corrupt. The very title is journalistically pretentious. But however much fraud or fancy may have gone into it, the Harlem Renaissance had its lasting merits. First, the actual fact of literary maturity and independence coming to ten or twenty Negro writers in a very short space of time is notable both as accomplishment and as example: from then on other prospective Negro writers had at least a model and a chance for success. Secondly, the simple race-pride satisfactions in the spectacle were genuine and enduring, the spectacle of Negro poets and novelists being published, acclaimed, and accepted as writers in the first American rank, whether they belonged there or not. And thirdly, it gave us Langston Hughes.

What *was* the Harlem Renaissance? Its social history —and it was, really, more a social than a literary event— may be traced best in records like the autobiographies of Langston Hughes (*The Big Sea*, 1940) or Claude

McKay (*A Long Way From Home*, 1937), or in James Weldon Johnson's *Black Manhattan* (1930) or McKay's *Harlem: Negro Metropolis* (1940).

Carl Van Vechten's *Nigger Heaven* (1926), the first Harlem-exposé novel (by a white man), is often blamed for starting the vogue, for introducing white society to the fun and games of Harlem cabaret slumming. It is a choice example of the flashy fad novel of the twenties, full of chichi chatter and decor and all the New Harlem clichés; but it is no worse, certainly, than the Negro versions that followed. It provided—as did Rudolph Fisher's *The Walls of Jericho*—a glossary of Harlem slang.

Other Harlem Negro novelists—Countee Cullen in *One Way to Heaven*, Wallace Thurman in *The Blacker the Berry* and *Infants of the Spring*, Claude McKay in *Home to Harlem*—indulged in the introverted fancy of drawing cartoons and sketches of their own literary milieu, even to quoting one another, and thus possess a kind of distorted documentary value. A key document-in-passage was the March 1925 Harlem number of *The Survey Graphic*, a display piece which proclaimed the existence of the "New Negro" and his works for all to hear. (This number was later expanded into Alain Locke's gaudy but useful anthology, *The New Negro*, 1925.) Other records may be found in the pages of the Negro press for the decade—*Crisis*, *Opportunity*, the big-city weeklies. And a number of responsible literary critics have probed the sources and assessed the creative products of the Harlem Renaissance.*

---

* See especially Hugh Gloster, *Negro Voices in American Fiction* (Chapel Hill, N.C., 1948), 101-195; and Robert Bone, *The Negro Novel in America* (New Haven, Conn., 1958), 51-108.

HARLEM AND THE MIDDLE CLASS:
THE NOVELS

The Harlem setting was an essential dynamic. America's major Negro metropolis scarcely existed in 1910, at the beginning of the great migrations of Southern Negroes. By 1925 it was, in James Weldon Johnson's proud words, "the greatest Negro city in the world." In the years between, the Negro settlement of uptown Manhattan took on the nature of an invasion. Owners fought with real-estate speculators, white and black; white tenants were dispossessed, put to flight, block by block. The banks gave in, about 1915, and began selling out their Harlem holdings to the immigrants. Within ten years, aided by the great waves of job-hunting Negroes through World War I, virtually all Harlem was in Negro hands. A city of 175,000 colored men had been established in what, from history's point of view, must have seemed like overnight. Chicago, Detroit, Philadelphia, Washington, Baltimore, all the Northern cities had their huge new ghettoes. But Harlem was the capital of Negro America, and it exercised an understandable fascination on a new generation of Negro writers.

Along with the new capital came, we are told, a "New Negro." The type was celebrated by Alain Locke in his introduction to *The New Negro*, a piece of militant, warfaring rhetoric. This New Negro was to assert himself proudly and independently, he insisted, to cast off the chains of servility and stereotype. Harlem was to be his glorious new spiritual home, the colorful symbol of his Coming of Age. He could now stand upright, and

41

celebrate his race—his African heritage, his music, his "Negro blood."

> He scans the world with calm and fearless
> eyes,
>> Conscious within of powers long since for-
>> got;
> At every step, new man-made barriers rise
>> To bar his progress—but he heeds them
>> not.
> He stands erect, though tempests round him
> crash,
>> Though thunder bursts and billows surge
>> and roll;
> He laughs and forges on, while lightnings
> flash
>> Along the rocky pathway to his goal.
> Impassive as a Sphinx, he stares ahead—
>> Foresees new empires rise and old ones fall;
> While caste-mad nations lust for blood to shed,
>> He sees God's finger writing on the wall.
> With soul awakened, wise and strong he
> stands,
> Holding his destiny within his hands.
> (James Edward McCall, "The New Negro")

> "Bliss was it in that dawn to be alive,
>> But to be young was very Heaven."

Wordsworth's lines are doubly applicable to this particular "dawn," for the poet was writing of the promise of the French Revolution, out of the bleak perspective of his own later abject disillusionment; the lines bear a heavy charge of irony. And nothing freezes the Harlem

Renaissance more into a past forever closed than a look back at the false, the pathetically high and unfulfilled hopes of its participants and observers. This is James Weldon Johnson, on the Harlem of 1925:

> It is not a slum or a fringe, it is located in the heart of Manhattan and occupies one of the most beautiful and healthful sections of the city. It is not a "quarter" of dilapidated tenements, but is made up of new-law apartments and handsome dwellings, with well-paved and well-lighted streets.

He writes of "magnificent Seventh Avenue," of New Negro millionaires. "I know of no place in the country where the feeling between the races is so cordial and at the same time so matter of fact and taken for granted," he declares; "Nor is there any unusual record of crime. . . . Will Harlem become merely a famous ghetto?" he rhetorically asks. "Will it become a point of friction between the races in New York?" He thought not.

Since the pride and the vision have proved to be illusory, it is no wonder that much of the literature based on them now seems to us equally hollow. However well intended or well written the Harlem novels may have been, they depicted only a two-dimensional facade, with the third dimension built of hope. The hopes have crumbled, the facade has turned grimy, and now all the charm, the high color and high spirits, the joyful assertion of the instinctual-voluptuary new life-style of Harlem are the record of a pathetic delusion.

The celebrity, during the Renaissance, of such non-literary figures as Paul Robeson, Ethel Waters, Louis Armstrong, Duke Ellington, Roland Hayes, Josephine Baker, and Bill Robinson may be accepted as genuine and earned; but the other side of the Harlem coin is represented by the cabaret-crawls of white Society up Lenox Avenue, the tremendous vogue for the Negro musical comedies of the decade—*Shuffle Along, Plantation Revue, Chocolate Dandies, Hot Chocolates:* an epochal cultural gap, as these titles make clear, divides the Harlem Renaissance from today.

But even in that dawn, there was much more to Harlem life than most of its recorders chose to show; they were painting not even its facade, but just the flaking top layer. Granted that Negro life in Harlem may have worsened perceptively in the interval, grown more tense and complex, even in 1925 it was not all brown jazz-babies and gin.

> Focusing upon carefree abandon, the Harlem school, like the plantation tradition, neglected the servitude. Except for brief glimpses, the drama of the workaday life, the struggles, the conflicts, are missing. And such definite features of Harlem life as the lines of the unemployed, the overcrowded schools, the delinquent children headed straight to petty crime, the surly resentment—all of these seeds that bore such bitter fruit in the Harlem riot —are conspicuously absent.*

The comparison with the Plantation Tradition supports our own perspective. For all the novelty of the Harlem school, the two traditions share much of a common irrelevance today, and, as Brown points out, for much the same reason. A few writers tried to reach beyond the colorful superficiality (and of course there was good reason to assert and accentuate the merely color-

---

* Sterling Brown, *The Negro in American Fiction*, Washington, 1937.

44

ful); to draw something more honest, more typical and complete. But too many were possessed by the artificial excitement, and by a view, ultimately, as outside and distant as Carl Van Vechten's. By their very literary stance—and this applies to the most famous, to Countee Cullen, Claude McKay, and Jean Toomer—they betrayed their own *difference* from the world they described. It is clear now that they did not, any of them, really understand even the Harlem of 1925, let alone the Harlem to come. For a picture of Harlem we can accept as more convincingly complete, one must wait for a wiser, maturer art: Ann Petry's *The Street* (1946), Langston Hughes' later lyrics or *The Sweet Flypaper of Life* (1955), James Baldwin's *Go Tell It on the Mountain* (1953) or "Sonny's Blues" (1965). To complete a portrait-in-depth of the Negro capital (no one's romantic dream city any more), I would add two other recent works: Warren Miller's *The Cool World* (1959), the finest Harlem novel so far, though a white man's; and Claude Brown's artless and awful autobiography, *Manchild in the Promised Land* (1965).

The excessive concern for a colorful surface, for a skin that has long since scaled off, is one of the two elements of a built-in obsolescence in most popular Harlem Renaissance novels. The other is their fixation with the social mores of the Negro middle class.

As the Negro writer grew more self-conscious and professional, he was met by a growing Negro reading public: an urban (even suburban) Northern Negro bourgeoisie, with all the dull limitations of its class. These were his readers, more often than not, and it was their little anxieties he was to dramatize, their little lives he was to make exciting, their fantasies he was to enact. The results could hardly be good novels—they are as commercial as the hot Harlem nocturnes, though aimed at a different audience of mediocrities. (This is not to say that one novel may not be written to both, as several were.) Thousands of similar domestic novels, social-status tragedies, were written, are being written, by forgotten and prosperous whites.

What this fixation affords to the critical surveyor is a great repetitive wash of dull, in-group, Negro-for-Negro novels through the twenties and thirties, detailing not "The Ethics of Living Jim Crow" but the Anxieties of Living High-Brown. However extensive a white reader's sympathies may be, these accounts can have for him little more than an anthropological interest, distant and exotic, like Gulliver's reports on the Lilliputians.

What sort of details are included? Primarily the skin-shade mania of Negro society, which is reiterated to a point of mental paralysis: "White is right," goes the jingle; "yellow, mellow; black, stand back."

From this basic standard come the "blue vein" circles of light-skinned aristocrats; the desirability of "high yellow" girls (as employees, dates, wives, mistresses, whores), and the hapless sufferings of the unwanted blacks, like Wallace Thurman's Emma Lou; the social rule that one always marries a paler type, and "breeds to light"—and then the tragedy of occasional genetic throwbacks in one's offspring.

Beyond, there lies the vast melodramatic realm of the "passing" theme, of the uncertainties of those light enough to cross over the color line—a source of tasteless fantasy plots from Charles Chesnutt to Nella Larsen, related to the popular "octoroon" melodramas of the mid-nineteenth century. The Negro social novels of the twenties and thirties are filled with details of skin-lightening preparations, the tragicomic possibilities of racial confusion, and Whitmanesque lists of the rich varieties of Negro color:

> Ancient black life rooted upon its base with all its fascinating new layers of brown, low-brown, high-brown, nut-brown, lemon, maroon, olive, mauve, gold, yellow balancing between black and white. Black reaching out beyond yellow. Almost-white on the brink of a change.
>
> (Claude McKay, *Home to Harlem*)

Of a similar source and quality is the anxiety for "good," i.e., non-kinky, white-like hair. I learned in at least four novels how to apply Madame Walker's goo with a stocking cap in order to straighten my hair. A colored woman would go to one of Madame's beauty parlors to have the kink ironed out instead. (Presumably the state of the art has advanced since then.)

At a further remove are the more commonplace details of a miniature society, which might seem hardly more bizarre than its white counterpart but for the fact that lightness of skin (and rightness of hair) is an important determinant of one's social rank. It *is* all a bit Lilliputian: all Society, let us grant, is artificial; but an imitation of an imitation comes closest to absurdity. Into this category of detail would fall the popular set pieces of Negro balls and socials; the details of fashions and costumes; and all the careful estimates of the social place of various churches, clubs, fraternal organizations, and neighborhoods. (Philadelphia, Washington, and Brooklyn all boasted a sort of old-guard Negro aristocracy, which sneered at the Harlem parvenus.) The phenomenon of the "dicty," or rising, class-conscious Negro, is viewed with scorn (or, more rarely, admiration) by almost *every* Negro writer of the period.

Add to this the endless intraracial wrangling over race pride and "assimilation," over the Negro press and the Negro pulpit, over "rising" and Heritage, over Africa and watermelons: it is all doubtless genuine, but it is also, to a white reader (and perhaps to some Negroes), very close and steamy, as would be the account of any subculture's taking itself too seriously, defining the world and its values exclusively in the terms of its own restrictive norms and concerns.

One can dislike all this inbred intensity, and yet grant the necessity of such concerns to the people involved. To the Negro writer and his world, such matters can quite conceivably assume a state of total and absolute consequence. They do in everyone's world.

One can dislike reading all these details, and yet further grant that the accounts may be useful. It is well, after all, for the white reader to know the inner details of the American Negro world. All such awareness of life "behind the wall" can have its value, if the white reader accepts the details not as exoticism or with condescension, but simply for what they are: the intramural behavior patterns of a small, semi-closed American society like his own.

Moreover, the frenzied little concerns of the Negro novelist's world, concerns over hair quality and skin shades and streets of residence, do at least take their ultimate source in the extramural anxiety, the race war: White is right. But such concerns can scarcely be regarded as a mark of adulthood, in any group. And reading of them, over and over, in these insular, middle-class novels, whether the concerns be viewed sympathetically or with scorn, is like reading a shelf-full of John O'Hara. It is all, finally, true to our own life or not, so inbred and childlike and petty, where one buys his clothes, by whom one is snubbed, to what club one can aspire.

One of the surest proofs of the maturity of Negro fiction since 1940 is the almost total absence of this area of argument, the supplanting of Jessie Fauset and Nella Larsen and Wallace Thurman by James Baldwin and Ralph Ellison and Ann Petry. (Dorothy West's *The Living Is Easy*, 1948, is the only notable hangover of this older and narrower breed.) The newer writers are obviously writing as men, for men, however much they may take their characters and issues from the worlds they know best; and not as middle-class Negroes for middle-class Negroes and the occasional white curiosity-seeking slummer.

If nothing else, though, the experience of these anxious little social novels may bring the white reader to share something of the sense of futile frenzy that still obviously dominates the lives of great numbers of Negroes. The reader's nervous disgust at reading, over and over, of these squirrel-cage torments of fruitless self-abuse may in fact be very like the endless gray anxiety of many provincial and unhappy Negroes.

Countee Cullen's *One Way to Heaven* (1932) adds to the Van Vechten model a tragic subplot, but it is still primarily an extravagant satire on the New Harlem culture, the literati, the Sugar Hill dicties, the white faddists, the New Negro propagandists. Rudolph Fisher's *The Walls of Jericho* (1928) is, for the most

49

part, trash: condescending, heavy-handed, and crude, it makes all Harlem seem a silly costume ball. Wallace Thurman's *Infants of the Spring* (1932) is a sordid satire on his fellow Harlem writers (the "Niggerati") and other Negro personalities. His *The Blacker the Berry* (1929) is a slightly better effort than the average, the product of a saner mind—not, at least, crude or coarse, just women's-magazine mediocre. It is *the* novel of intraracial color mania, full of bitter talk by Negroes about The Problem. Arna Bontemps' *God Sends Sunday* (1931) does not actually deal with Harlem or the Renaissance, but seizes a sugary, harmless version of its spirit and spreads it over the ragtime-and-cakewalk era in New Orleans and St. Louis.

Claude McKay disgusted DuBois and his moralist friends with a flamboyant pageant of the depraved Harlem underground, *Home to Harlem*, (1928) (he took the same crowd to Marseilles for a second novel, *Banjo*, the following year). DuBois' strictures may have been wrong-headed ("The Debauched Tenth," he called McKay's people), but the novels do not merit defense. McKay was a doctrinaire eroticist (and eventually Marxist) whose plotless works were made up of "pure voluptuous jazzing," of "pagan abandon," of orgies of one sort or another—razor fights, raids, drunken whores in orange silk dresses. One cannot help but agree with DuBois' conjecture of their *épater le* (*blanc*) *bourgeois* intentions.

Other than Wallace Thurman, the major Negro novelists of middle-class society during the period were Nella Larsen and Jessie Fauset. Nella Larsen's novels (*Quicksand*, 1928; *Passing*, 1929) show a certain nervous accuracy in their dramatizations of female psychology, but none of Jessie Fauset's four works rises above the stuffy, tiny-minded circulating-library norm. Her vapidly genteel lace-curtain romances, however (with a dash added of the melodrama of color), were once held up by the DuBois crowd as an example of what tasteful things Negro novels could be.

Three fictional works of the period, for three different reasons, should be exempted from this blanket dismissal: George Schuyler's *Black No More* (1931), Langston Hughes' *Not Without Laughter* (1930), and Jean Toomer's *Cane* (1923), which I shall discuss later on with his poetry.

I would exempt Schuyler's fantasy because, though broad, it is genuinely funny, the best satire to come out of the race war before *Purlie Victorious*. "Black-No-More," in the novel, is a gland treatment which turns Negroes into whites, changing all racial characteristics irrevocably. It sweeps the country, sends white America into a panic, upsets the social, political, and economic systems, and puts Negro leaders out of their jobs. In the end, a tantalizing new balance is restored with the discovery that *real* whites are slightly darker than chemical ones.

Schuyler writes flabbily, sad to say, without control —he was a muckraking journalist by profession—and dilutes the high potential of his provocative idea. His artillery is aimed every which way, and his plot line swoops from effective quasi-realism to outrageous burlesque. The mode, if not the intelligence, is comparable to that of Joseph Heller's *Catch-22*. In both cases the subjects—race war and "real" war—were well met by the wild, spleenful anarchy of attack. One such work per generation would be good for the national health.

51

Langston Hughes' fiction I will mention again in Chapter VII. But *Not Without Laughter* deserves notice here as an antidote to the many shrill and artificial Harlem Renaissance novels.

It is not easy to define Hughes' achievement without making him sound corny or soft. Formulations of his work come out like Faulkner's stodgy explanations of his own novels, even to the motifs of "affirmation" and "endurance." *Not Without Laughter* belongs with the fiction of its simpler time. It is a gentle sequence of well-sketched social views, like so many Negro novels of the period—the family gatherings, the colored ball, the pool hall. It even includes the standard caricature of the Episcopalian, anti-watermelon dicty.

Its special value, like that of DuBois' social essays, lies in its completeness and truth, its control and wide humanity. It is probably the most genuine inside view of Negro life available in the fiction of the period, comparable to later works like Ann Petry's. Like almost all of Hughes' work it is sad, to a degree, but never violent or bitter; it is touching, but never falsely sentimental. It is very small, really, in outline—a collection of the more or less connected stories of a family of very average, very attractive small-town Negroes in Kansas; but the stories flow with the warmth of genuine life.

SERIOUSNESS, SELF-IDENTITY, AND MOTHER AFRICA: THE POETS

The Harlem Renaissance novelists rode to fame, for the most part, on transient concerns, now as dated as their boxy orange bindings with art-nouveau lettering.

The poets of the Renaissance, a quite different phenomenon, took themselves and their art far more seriously. (More seriously even than "themselves as novelists," since many were both.) They came closer to acting as independent, even aggressively independent, artists. Their range of style and experiment, their variety of subject and manner are more a dark reflection-in-little of the whole modernist foment of the decade, the decade of Picasso and Stravinsky (and, not irrelevantly, of the discovery of African Negro sculpture). If the novelists reproduce, in a sort of toy version, the period of Fitzgerald and Sinclair Lewis, of hip flasks and Babbitts, the poets reflect the concerns of the Sandburgs and Pounds and Amy Lowells. They were genuine Bohemians, hard-working artists doing their individual best, as poets are likely to be. Langston Hughes, properly, wrote their manifesto, their declaration of independence.

> We younger Negro artists who create now intend to express our individual dark-skinned selves without fear or shame. If the white people are pleased, we are glad. If they are not, it doesn't matter. We know we are beautiful, and ugly too. The tom-tom cries and the tom-tom laughs. If colored people are pleased, we are glad. If they are not, their displeasure doesn't matter either. We build our temples for tomorrow, strong as we know them, and we stand on the top of the mountain, free within ourselves.
> (Langston Hughes, "The Negro Artist and the Racial Mountain")

The four most discussed Negro poets of the period, Jean Toomer, Countee Cullen, Claude McKay, and

Langston Hughes, were all genuine poets of the new dispensation, not mere imitators or versemakers. Theirs is, really, the first American Negro writing one can judge absolutely, with no necessary reference to its context. They are better than the earlier Negro poets not because they are New Negroes, but because American poetry itself grew up in the 1920's, and they were there. Of the four, even the least worthy is of serious consequence, by comparison with earlier names in our survey. But only one has earned a place in the minor ranks of important *American* poets, regardless of race, creed, or color.

Langston Hughes belongs, fairly, at least as much in my discussion of the poets of present generation, in Chapter V—the generation since 1940—as in these back files of the Harlem Renaissance. At sixty-four, after thirty books and a "Langston Hughes Reader," he remains the most impressive, durable, and prolific Negro writer in America. His voice is as sure, his manner as original, his position as secure as, say, Edwin Arlington Robinson's or Robinson Jeffers'. He is the one sure Negro classic, more certain of permanence than even Baldwin or Ellison or Wright. By molding his verse always on the sounds of Negro talk, the rhythms of Negro music, by retaining his own keen honesty and directness, his poetic sense and ironic intelligence, he has maintained through four decades a readable newness distinctly his own. His finest book of poetry, *Montage of a Dream Deferred*, was written in the bop mode of the early fifties. In his latest work, designed for jazz readings in the sixties, he plays new games with typography, with inset prose dialogue, with dual columns of counterpointed verse. Hughes is a true professional, like the hero of his fictions only deceptively "Simple." Younger artists and jazzmen, now that he is a Personality, a member of the National Institute, may suspect him of a degree of condescension, even conscious fraud. But the voice, at least, remains genuine. He has earned the tributes of translation and imitation, and has produced, for the white reader, a convincing, singing source book on the emotional life-style of the lower-class urban Negro in America, as valid as the blues.

Countee Cullen is a queer twentieth-century example of an English traditionalist, "loving the measured line and skillful rhyme," a good example of what becomes of a talent too rooted in the past. He could carve easily metered, run-on lines with a sophisticated and polished placing of words, an exact and unforced precision of accent, in the best manner of Tennyson or Keats. He could actually build sonnets, sonnets that worked, crisply and easily, on the stock sixteenth-century Renaissance love themes; little Herricky trifles on enrubied and palpitant hearts; or ballad-measure stanzas of a tired young aesthete's longing for death. He believed in Beauty, sang to Shelley and Keats ("And You and I, shall we be still,/ John Keats, while Beauty summons us"), and altogether summons up the image of a flowing-tie, nineteenth-century poet. As the earlier Negro versemakers were bad nineteenth-century poets, Countee Cullen was a fairly good one.

But there are limitations to such precious, archaic skills. The diction (e.g., "sable breast") is bound to seem at times simply false. The style, so inadequately suited to his contemporary or even commonplace subjects, forces one to regard him not as an honest spokesman, but as a detached exquisite, a builder of poems, crafting elegant little reliquaries for his themes. The race-protest poems, in particular, come out sounding too frail and wood-windy, too mellow and suave. He had sipped of the New Harlem wine, and tried very hard to insist on his own "pagan blood"; but the false primitivism, the hopeful, distant assertion of his Congo heritage is unpleasantly clear:

> Why should he deem it pure mischance
> A son of his is fain
> To do a naked tribal dance
> Each time he hears the rain?

He should at least be given credit for "Heritage" (along with three or four other rereadable poems, "A Brown Girl Dead," "Incident," "Variations on a Theme"), the lead-off piece of the African heritage revival among New Negroes, which has never entirely died. Perhaps because I believe that no really intelligent American Negro could ever fall for the African heritage line (though many have)—there is so evidently no real contact between the cultures, the Ashanti warrior-kings are like ancestors bought from a genealogist or an art gallery, the whole jungle-blood affair reeks of adolescent daydreaming—I cannot take too seriously any of the great run of Negro poems or statements on the theme. But Cullen's effort is a decent, drumbeating, rollicking thing, with a few lines ("the unremittent beat/Made by cruel padded feet/Walking through my body's street") that come near to convincing.

Claude McKay, as a poet, is most kindly served by reading a few of his strongest poems, or even selected lines. The more thoroughly one studies his work, the more disagreeably McKay is revealed as the small-souled declamatory propagandist we meet in his novels. The best poems from his angry series of race-war sonnets ("Baptism," "If We Must Die," "Outcast," "Like a Strong Tree," "The White House") convey a bitter, masculine, very personal strength, a kind of enlightened crimson rant: the man loves to hate, and has objects worth hating.

There is nothing new or experimental about his efforts. At its best (or at the reader's most tolerant) his work seems to have a kind of harsh, proud seventeenth-century vigor, like Milton's sonnet "On the Late Massacre in Piedmont" ("Avenge, O Lord, thy slaughtered saints"). From another point of view, though, the diction may be seen as a kind of archaic British bluster ("O let us nobly die," "Kinsmen," "bend the knee," "clime," "making their mock at our accursed lot"); the best-known of his poems was once quoted by Churchill.

His strength *is* in his anger, in the fury of his rhythms and images and diction; his weakness lies in his small-mindedness and poetic inability. He writes in chunky, aggressively iambic, end-stopped pentameters, deep-chested rhetorical lines of accusation and defiance, full of mouth-filling vowels and chopped consonants. He will make a dozen bad mistakes per sonnet, and dip to all forms of archaism and syntactic ineptitude to crash his way out of a poem ("From dulcet thoughts of you my guts are twisted"). Looked at too closely, the ideas behind his angry rhetoric often show as incoherent black-racist propaganda. He is not a pleasant sort.

But often his verse can be carried along by the simple constant fire of his diction. And in his most successful angry sonnets, a small idea is sublimed into one compulsive image, a fine unity of image and structure pulls the whole together, and he is left with no room for the usual archaisms of diction or clumsiness of rhythm.

I would mention too his one most horrible, most captivating poem, "The Desolate City," a potent nightmare allegory of the spirit as a city in plague, glutted with fine images of decay; and especially his "Amoroso" sequence of sex poems, more convincingly passionate than anything of Swinburne's. These are extraordinary things, celebrations of real copulations arguably better than his race-war sonnets. That none of the Negro anthologies includes them among his works is an interesting testimony to their effect.

Jean Toomer's career is still wrapped in foggy mystery: he wrote one esoteric work, difficult to grasp, define, and assess; he was associated with one of the more advanced white modernist cults, and adopted and taught Russian mysticism; and then he suddenly declared himself white, and disappeared.

His book, *Cane* (1923), is composed of fourteen prose pieces, ranging from two- and four-page sketches, to "Kabnis," an eighty-three-page *nouvelle;* and fifteen detached poems set in between. About half the "stories" have tiny lyric refrains tucked inside them as well.

The prose pieces in the first section of the book are detached vignettes of high female sexuality among the Negro peasants of the Dixie Pike. They are drawn with the new honest artfulness of the Stein-Anderson-Hemingway tradition, so crisp and icily succinct that the characters seem bloodless and ghostly, for all the fury of their indicated lives, all style and tone and sug-

gestion. It is into this section that Toomer's finest poems
are set—"Song of the Son," "Georgia Dusk," "Portrait
in Georgia"—poems which reveal a great deal about his
viewpoint and method. They are the most freely experimental Negro poems of the generation, far freer even
than Langston Hughes' games with the rhythms of jazz
and conversation. They view Southern Negro life with a
chilling objectivity ("so objective he might not be a
Negro," an early critic prophetically observed). Common things are seen as if through a strangely neurotic
vision, transformed into his own kind of nightmare.

> Hair—braided chestnut, coiled like a lynch-
>   er's rope,
> Eyes—fagots,
> Lips—old scars, or the first red blisters,
> Breath—the last sweet scent of cane,
> And her slim body, white as the ash of black
>   flesh after flame.

In "Song of the Son" he tries to identify himself
with the Georgia soil, but the very effort makes clear
his distant view; the view of a sophisticated surrealist
among an alien peasantry, a peasantry he transforms
into something duskily primeval.

> O Negro slaves, dark purple ripened plums,
> Squeezed, and bursting in the pine-wood air,
> Passing, before they stripped the old tree bare
> One plum was saved for me, one seed be-
>   comes
>
> An everlasting song, a singing tree,
> Caroling softly souls of slavery,

What they were, and what they are to me,
Caroling softly souls of slavery.

The prose pieces of the second section support this
view, though now his bony surrealist's objectivity is
transferred to Northern urban Negroes. In the two key
stories, "Box Seat" and "Bona and Paul," he runs hot
wires of anti-realism beneath a surface of realistic
events, somewhat in the manner of Malcolm Lowry or
John Hawkes, to imply a strange neurotic derangement
in his characters. It is primarily a matter of imagery:

> Through the cement floor her strong roots sink
> down. They spread under the asphalt streets.
> Dreaming, the streets roll over on their bellies,
> and suck their glossy health from them. Her
> strong roots sink down and spread under the river
> and disappear in blood-lines that waver south.
> Her roots shoot down. Dan's hands follow them.
> Roots throb. . . .

The long story "Kabnis" that makes up the third
part is crafted of nervous images and a strong sense
of interior pain. The underground cellar symbolism is
disturbing, as is, again, the utter objectivity of the nar-
ration. But the story drifts off into a hazy poetic incoherence, and—like most of the book, finally—is too
insubstantial to be remembered. For all that, the book
should really be allowed to come back into print.

After these four poets, I would include in a Harlem
Renaissance anthology only two other poems: Waring
Cuney's "No Images" (1926),

She does not know
Her beauty,
She thinks her brown body
Has no glory.
If she could dance
Naked,
Under palm trees
And see her image in the river
She would know.

But there are no palm trees
On the street
And dish water gives back no images,

and at least some parts of Frank Horne's "Letters Found Near a Suicide" (1925).

AFTER THE RENAISSANCE

"That spring for me (and, I guess, all of us)," wrote Langston Hughes of 1930, "was the end of the Harlem Renaissance. We were no longer in vogue, anyway, we Negroes. Sophisticated New Yorkers turned to Noel Coward. Colored actors began to go hungry, publishers politely rejected new manuscripts, and patrons found new uses for their money." The Depression, he wrote, "sent Negroes, white folks and all rolling down the hills toward the Works Progress Administration."

Some of the works I have mentioned do spill over past 1930, but there was, in general, a decided drying-up of the spring of Negro writing in the thirties. A few new poets emerge, three or four drab Depression-era

61

novels are published, Negro playwrights begin to get a hearing. But there is nothing to compare with the fever of the twenties, or even with the more respectable works of the Gilded Age: let alone with the new explosion that began with *Native Son* in 1940, itself a late Depression child. The best work of the period by a Negro was Richard Wright's collection of stories, *Uncle Tom's Children* (1938), which I will discuss along with his other work in Chapter VI.

Two leading Negro intellectuals, Arna Bontemps and Sterling Brown, professors, critics, and anthologists of Negro culture, began their poetic careers in the thirties. Bontemps' "Southern Mansion," with its eerily clanking slavery memories, is a small must for everyone's collection: a few of his humble and exact after-love poems deserve a place as well. Brown, a professor at Howard University, made a vigorous and intelligent attempt to do for the Southern Negro what Langston Hughes had done for the Northern, in a series of ballad-like narrative tales of racial protest: chants, chain-gang songs, stories, and the like. His irony was sharp, his ideas were exciting; he was one of the first protestors-in-verse (and there were many) to pay heed to the basic demands of good poetry. Some of his poems, with their hammer-driving freedoms, their guitar-picking rhythms, have the poignant authenticity of folk song. He lacked, unfortunately, any real organic verbal skill, so his poetry still resides more in his ideas, in the effects of underplayed indirection, than in the total achievement. But it was right for the time, and it remains a strong indictment.

Frank Davis, a journalist, editor, and professional Negro Leader, began with very angry protest stuff—

Of course
There is no intermingling socially
Between the races
Such is absolutely unthinkable
Oh my yes
Still
At regular intervals
The wife of Mobtown's mayor
Sees an Atlanta specialist
For syphillis contracted from her husband
Who got it from their young mulatto cook
Who was infected by the chief of police
Who received it from his washerwoman
Who was made diseased by the shiftless son
Of the section's richest planter
One night before
He led the pack that hanged
The black bastard who broke into
A farm woman's bedroom—
But
As was mentioned before
There is no intermingling socially . . .

then moved through a phase of hard imagism; but his security for posterity lies in a few neat little bitter comic portrait poems of the black bourgeoisie.

The novels of the period, other than Arna Bontemps' two dismal ventures into "historical fiction," convey something of the dusty, distant drabness of that decade. Zora Hurston and George Wylie Henderson both returned to the Southern Negro peasantry; William Attaway wrote an odd, elusive novel about jobless white drifters. There is something very dutiful and serious about the work of all three, and I suspect the writing of them to have been as joyless as the reading.

The Negro, the American exotic, has been a favorite theme in the white theater almost from its start, from minstrel shows and octoroon melodramas to the "Chocolate Drops" musical revues and Marxist protest plays of the twenties and thirties. In the former decade especially, a tremendous vogue ran from *The Emperor Jones* through *Porgy* to *Green Pastures*. But almost nothing was heard on their own theme from *Negro* playwrights before the 1930's. This silence is understandable, perhaps, considering that a serious Negro theater audience was almost nonexistent (they laughed *The Emperor Jones* out of Harlem) and that chances for the stage experience necessary to develop the particular skills of theatrical writing were rare. James Weldon Johnson and Paul Dunbar had both written for the Negro musical stage back in the ragtime era, but after them there is nothing of even minor note before Hall Johnson's revivalist spectacle, *Run Little Children*, of 1933.

Langston Hughes collaborated on *Mulatto* in 1935, a simple (and successful) modern melodrama of the South, whose hero has interesting correspondences with Richard Henry of Baldwin's *Blues for Mister Charlie*. His folk comedies of the urban Negro are for the most part diluted versions of his stories, and his propagandist "pageants" and cantatas are something other than literature. Several other leading Harlem writers tried their hands at playwriting—Arna Bontemps, Countee Cullen, Rudolph Fisher, Wallace Thurman—but nothing memorable resulted, despite the boost of the Federal Theatre Project. Orson Welles directed, under its auspices, a stage version of Wright's *Native Son* in 1940; dedicated school playwrights like Randolph Edmonds and Willis Richardson tried hard to establish a "Negro Theater"; and two or three younger playwrights have come up in off-Broadway and on television and films in the forties and fifties. But one would not be unfair in dating the emergence of a serious and mature Negro theater in America from 1959, the date of Lorraine Hansberry's *A Raisin in the Sun.*

IV
NEGRO WRITERS TODAY:
THE PLAYWRIGHTS

It should not be hard to see why I draw so firm a line between Negro writing in America before 1940, and that after. If the race war in America has been going on for a hundred years or more, it was not really on in earnest, not a war between equal adversaries, before that time. It is this *war* element, this attack, and with it a new kind of truth to suit a new situation, that so distinguishes the Negro literature of our day. Before 1940—which is of course a symbolic, not an absolute line—both parties were laboring under gross delusions, and few Negroes were sufficiently emancipated and mature to tell the whole truth, or strong enough to hit back.

The cataclysmic reversals in race relations within the last twenty-five years have made a great deal of the writing I have been discussing in the last two chapters of considerable irrelevance. It is not so much that it is *bad*, though most of it is; or that it is uninteresting, since the cultural historian would not find it so; but simply that it is irrelevant. The writers of the twenties, especially, seem now so parochial, so quaintly sure of their modernism. (So, of course, may we.) Langston Hughes alone has survived by adapting. There was so much falseness in the American's view of the Negro—and not only in the white man's Aunt Dinah and Rochester and Amos 'n' Andy, but also in the Negro's *own* view—that the crack *had* to be something as extreme and explosive as *Native Son*.

Most of the Negro literature before 1940 has remained in print on its race-pride value alone, its value for Negro education and Negro self-celebration. Colored schools are named for Phillis Wheatley; Richard Bardolph (in *The Negro Vanguard*) mentions a young Midwestern Negro writer of the forties who "was so remote from Negro life that she had not heard of . . . Paul Laurence Dunbar until she was halfway through college." I had not heard of him until last year. It is interesting to compare this phenomenon with the similar pride, parental and uncritical, lavished by many of the new black African countries on *their* writers. It is obviously a useful sentiment for under-dog cultures.

Even the best Negro writing of the "Dark Ages" is now of primarily historical importance. It reflects a small, adolescent, and isolationist America. The race war then beginning was barbarically simple and hopelessly one-sided. Medieval instances of brutality, near-pogroms were commonplace. It is good to remember how it all began, but also to reflect how much has changed.

The twenties substituted a ghetto mentality for a feudal mentality, but the writing was still detached and exotic. The in-group subcultural portraits, the neo-romanticism of Harlem and the African heritage have too little bearing on interracial realities. More realistic views, more angry protests grew up in the interim years, but the outspoken depiction of a war between equals only emerged from the new pressures and new situations of the late Depression, the Second World

War, and especially the postwar period. American Negroes are no longer shown as the suffering Hebrew children of the spirituals, but as well-armed adversaries.

With the bombs still bursting in air, it is clear that we have not reached a final stage. However strong, even finished one may regard the American Negro writing of this generation, there is every reason to expect that it, too, will seem irrelevant from a later perspective. Let us not fall into the trap of confessing everyone's contingency but our own. The very quality of brittle excess, the strident, self-mocking, sex-obsessed quality of the art of the sixties is very soon going to type it *as* "The Art of the Sixties." The virulent anti-Uncle Tomism of the New Negro (or "Newer Negro"?) has about it the shrillness and militancy of a passing battle. The rejection of all the suspect elements in the American Negro past—the spirituals, the "uplift" theme, the myth of Endurance, traditional Negro Christianity—all this will probably pass. There may even come a day, probably two hundred years from now when we are all beige, when plantation-darky stories will be no more intolerable or embarrassing to us than class-structured eighteenth-century novels are today.

There are four Negro playwrights of note in the contemporary American theater: Lorraine Hansberry, Ossie Davis, James Baldwin, and LeRoi Jones.* Since

---

* Martin Duberman's *In White America* (1964) also deserves mention. Although it is neither a play nor by a Negro, this series of documentary readings from the Negro's past is dramatic, moving, and useful. I would especially draw attention to Senator ("Pitchfork") Ben Tillman's speech in defense of lynching of 1907, pp. 51-52.

the theater is as much a social event as an art form, it provides the "race-war" artist with the perfect battleground for his explosions. The confrontation between black playwright and white audience is literally face to face. His accusations, here, will be seen and heard, not just read and imagined. Every device of theatrical spectacle is at hand for the Negro artist and his company to put to use. The effect, conceivably, could be stunning —more total, more irresistibly all-involving than that of any novel or poem read quietly in the study. Here, it would seem, is the perfect medium for the race-war writer. Jean Genet (an outsider for other reasons than race) set an obvious pattern for American Negro playwrights with the spectacle, the audience abuse, the role confusion of his own race-war play, *The Blacks*.

The social-event element, however, works two ways. If in one sense the white auditor is more open, more vulnerable than while reading alone, in another he is more protected, more resistant: he is "padded" by the fellow audience members of his race, by his spouse or companion, by the whole soft urban ritual of Going to the Theater. It is almost impossible for a Negro playwright to penetrate the cocoon of gentility that clings around most white spectators. LeRoi Jones has mocked the foolish giggles and ritual applause afforded his plays by white audiences he intends to insult. A far more honest, more appreciative gesture, he feels, would be to tramp out in disgust; or at least to sit silent. The director of the American Society of African Culture noted, with how much irony I do not know, that while Lorraine Hansberry's *A Raisin in the Sun* is social protest, "it is such a consummate work of art that the objects of the protest applaud it vigorously each night on Broadway."

At each intermission, and especially at the final curtain, white auditors are afforded the rich and windy release of small talk, which inevitably stays small. They can—at least for the moment—deflect the intended Negro whip with grace and serenity, far more effectively than could the solitary white reader, imprisoned with a demon author in his own imagination. They can try, at least, by comparing decorous opinions with their fellows, to dissolve the impact of the experience into some safe common denominator. The playwright must probably rest content with the hope that enough shrapnel shreds of his missile have penetrated, despite all precautions, into the auditors' unconscious minds, to rankle and fester later on; or that a few white playgoers still attend the theater alone, in fact or in spirit.

In any case, no Negro playwright except LeRoi Jones has even begun yet to take advantage of the dynamic potential of the living theater, in the manner initiated by Genet. Lorraine Hansberry's *A Raisin in the Sun* (New York Drama Critics' Circle Award, 1959) is a conventional social-realist drama, the short story of an embattled Negro family in Chicago's Black Belt, and their small unsatisfied dreams. It borrows its title from Langston Hughes:

What happens to a dream deferred?
Does it dry up
like a raisin in the sun?
Or fester like a sore—
And then run?

70

Does it stink like rotten meat?
Or crust and sugar over—
like a syrupy sweet?

Maybe it just sags
like a heavy load.

Or does it explode?

In the manner of many novels, it manages to suggest
the white man's oppression of the Negro in Northern
slums, through the domestic tensions and frustrations
that are its result. To a simple, effective plot are added
strong doses of African nationalism, assimilationist
propaganda, Uncle Tomism, wage slavery, white residential prejudice, and other common elements of the
Negro experience. An active, theatrical sound arises
from the taut pull of family discords, which remains
strong throughout the play. The work may be too
straightforward, in the end, too loving and simple and
direct to wound effectively, though it may teach something of the inner pressure of Negro life. Despite some
difficult moments, everything *does* come comfortably
right in the end, and even a white audience may be left
safely content. This "safe" play, it is worth noting, was
a Broadway and Hollywood success. Miss Hansberry's
second play (and last; she died of cancer in 1964 at the
age of thirty-four), *The Sign in Sidney Brustein's Window*, ran briefly in New York in 1964, and then toured
the country. It is a shrill, vigorous, semi-comic display
of (again) intrapersonal tensions, here among a mixed
crowd of Greenwich Village Bohemians, mostly white,

all living on the edges of their nerves. The raspy verbal
violence, the domestic discord, recall, as they did in
Raisin, an early John Osborne.

Ossie Davis' *Purlie Victorious* (1961; transferred
almost directly to the screen as *Gone Are the Days*)
was a few years ahead of its time. Despite an underground notoriety, it did not come into its own until the
new wave of satire, British and American, caught up
with it just a few years ago. It is the first full-length
race-war satire, conceived in the wide-open, nothing-
sacred vein of *Beyond the Fringe, Dr. Strangelove,* and
TW3, with a warm extravagance of its own. Though
its plot is the merest patch-up, the play is robust and
theatrical, and bursting with rich racial *double-enten-
dres*. Mr. Davis composed the word-drunken part of
Reverend Purlie to suit his own exuberant talents; God-
frey Cambridge, one of the best new Negro comedians,
took the part of a classic two-faced Uncle Tom who
sings slavery songs to his master. The fact that so suc-
cessfully comic, so healthfully double-edged a take-off
on racial oppression and the Civil Rights struggle could
be written and produced is one of the surest signs of
the maturity of Negro art. Every sugary Deep South
lie, every hoary delusion and institution is deftly
mocked in the play; its white folks are all patent fools.
This is clearly a Negroes' show, for Negroes to laugh
at; the jokes are all theirs. But white viewers, too, if
they are ready for it, can relish its sanity.

James Baldwin has followed the traditional pattern
of the Man of Letters, the Man of Letters with a message, in utilizing almost every means of verbal expression to convey his warnings. But almost anyone so
committed to directness of statement is likely to find the

odd exigencies of theater more a hindrance than a help. One can tell the truth in novels, especially novels like Baldwin's, more or less directly; one must tell the truth in social essays. But a play is made up fundamentally of the lies of other people's lives. The truth is never in the parts, but in the sum, never stated, but experienced. In *The Amen Corner* (1953; New York production, 1965), a play derived, to some degree, from the same childhood experience as *Go Tell It on the Mountain*, Baldwin was able to attain something of the stark sincerity of that memoir-novel, despite an excess of rhetoric over plot. But his more ambitious attempt, *Blues for Mister Charlie* (1964), betrays serious imaginative disability.

The play was obviously intended as an explosive race-war document of the sort I have described, "an attempt," as one reviewer put it, "to give the Caucasians in the audience a white inferiority complex." With some Caucasians the attempt succeeded all too easily, and reviewers paid pious acknowledgments to the justice of Baldwin's anger. But it is an essay in artless bullying, not a play. Its wicked South is faked, its white villains are flat collages of prejudice-clichés—and this despite Baldwin's professed moral experiment (in the wake of the Medgar Evars murder), his generous attempt to imagine a Southern lynch-killer as a human being. There are playable, even moving moments, bits of ritual drama ("Blacktown" talks to "Whitetown"), intriguing shifts back and forth in time. But the dialogue, for the most part, is hopeless: faked banter, faked poetry, doctrinaire racism, dated slang, all conflated with artificial violence and obscenity. The play rarely comes to life, enough life to hurt a serious

73

listener, because Baldwin lacked either the skill or the patience to imagine completely the place, the story, or the people. If it is not so absolutely a dud as LeRoi Jones' *The Slave*, it is enough so to convince one that Baldwin is no playwright—he has difficulty imagining anyone not Baldwin. It provides a perfect example of the relinquishing of judgment by an undiscerning and intimidated white audience.

The later bill of LeRoi Jones' two one-act plays, *The Toilet* and *The Slave* (1964), is not his major effort. *The Toilet* is a violent and attention-grabbing little pop-art documentary of the actions and talk, much of it honestly obscene, in the boys' toilet of a city high school. A white boy, accused of homosexual advances to a Negro, is beaten up by a gang of the latter's fellows as part of the morning's business. The play deftly ends with a pathetic tableau of the two boys; the white boy had not been mistaken. Outside of the final effect, the play's major strength lies in its sense of menace. It is otherwise loose, even sloppy, and Jones' noble try at pure illusionism—the notion that this is, in fact, real life we are watching, unrehearsed and unacted, even to his director's use of "real amateurs" onstage—is theoretically hopeless. Our attention may indeed be riveted by the high degree of "tape recorder" realism; but there is always, up there behind the footlights, that Invisible Plastic Shield.

The Slave, on the other hand, is a blatant, unmodulated scream of racial abuse; its primary purpose, one assumes, was authorial self-gratification. A maniacal Negro gunman shrieks insults at a white couple for an hour, while a race riot of holocaustic proportions sup-

74

posedly rages outside. He beats them, spits on them, forces them to crawl, finally shoots them.

> My country tis of thee, sweet land of liberty (*screams off key like a drunken opera singer*). Well, let's say liberty and ignorant vomiting faggot professors . . . Right, lady? Isn't that right? I mean you ought to know, cause you went out of your way to marry one . . .
>
> Huh? Huh? And then fed the thing my children. (*He reaches stiffly out and pushes her . . . Grace falls back . . .*)

"Ritual drama, we used to call it at the university." "Mr. Vessels is playing the mad scene from *Native Son*." The stopper to one argument, a dramatic moment typical of the play's subtlety, is: "Go and fuck yourself." It is so devoid of conflict, of dramatic content— the whites are such pappy, wish-fulfilling projections ("Professor No-Dick"), the gunman such a sick, simple noise, that the only reasonable response, white or black, is one of embarrassed and annoyed detachment. Which, perhaps, is what Jones wanted.

The Dutchman ("Obie"—off-Broadway—award for 1963-64) is quite another matter. It may be the most important imaginative literary document of the American race war since *Native Son*. And it works. Jones has here channeled his hate equally into *two* antagonists, a young Negro boy and the violent white female (a stunning part for an actress) who accosts him on a New York subway, and has managed to create in their encounter one of the more genuine and irresistible conflicts of the modern stage.

The dialogue between the two is almost perfect. It

75

conveys the shrill, sharp, absolutely open insult-trading of cool modern neurotics, hiding nothing except everything, all very uptight New Yorky 1964. And just beneath it, one can *feel* the peeled-grape hypersensitivity, the heading-for-a-crackup comic tension.

> LULA: And why're you wearing a jacket and tie like that? Did your people ever burn witches or start revolutions over the price of tea? Boy, those narrow-shoulder clothes come from a tradition you ought to feel oppressed by. . . . Your grandfather was a slave, he didn't go to Harvard.
>
> CLAY: My grandfather was a night watchman.
>
> LULA: And you went to a colored college where everybody thought they were Averell Harriman.
>
> CLAY: All except me.
>
> LULA: And who did you think you were? Who do you think you are now?
>
> CLAY: Well, in college I thought I was Beaudelaire. But I've slowed down since.
>
> LULA: I'll bet you never once thought you were a black nigger.

It has its share of Becketty nonsense ("What's my name?" "Morris the Hyena." "The famous woman poet?" "The same."), of forced "funny" laughter, of open confessions of the sick role-playing they are doing, we are doing, everyone is doing; and of full-stop ritual insults in the manner of Edward Albee—the play originally shared a bill with *The Zoo Story*, making an exhausting evening's theater—wanting only Albee's unerring sense of theatrical rhythm. The agon, the struggle, subsists entirely in the vicious, *non sequitur* conversational game. The sense of danger lies in Clay's attempts to keep up, to hold his own, to stay resilient and responsive before this redheaded harridan, and prevent the raspy human comedy from collapsing into chaos.

For a while he keeps up, and the flood is held off. Then Lula wriggles "twist-like" through the subway train, past eye-averting passengers (the stage directions are as imaginative as the text); demands sex from Clay here and now; and then explodes out in exorcising racial insult. The dam bursts.

> You middle-class black bastard. Forget your social-working mother for a few seconds and let's knock stomachs. Clay, you liver-lipped white man. You would be Christian. You ain't no nigger, you're just a dirty white man. Screw yourself. Uncle Tom. Uncle Thomas Woolly-head . . . Let the white man hump his ol' mama, and he jes' shuffle off in the woods and hide his gentle gray head. (*Some of the other riders are laughing* . . .)

As the only dramatic act possible, he slaps her, loudly; then replies with a ten-minute explanation of the race-war rules. He gains the upper hand—the audience, hopefully, has by this time been dragooned into participation—but decides not to kill her, and prepares to leave. She stabs him, abruptly, orders the other passengers to throw the body off the train, then get off. They do. "She takes out a note book and makes a quick scribbling note." Another young Negro enters the car. She stares after him. Curtain.

In performance, certain difficulties with the play

become manifest, difficulties which could, conceivably, be overcome by an extraordinarily skilled director and cast.* Pre-eminent is that of modulating, somehow, from the "safe" to the "unsafe" lines, finding a pace and breath for the play that can encompass its sudden and extreme variations of effect, without the jarring jerkiness that disengages a spectator's response. The actors, too—especially the Negro—must find some means of enlivening their longer, more doctrinaire speeches.

Audience response itself will always remain a problem with Jones' efforts. Everyone in the theater seems to encase himself, to hold himself off, to *refuse* so to be hit. They slyly watch their neighbors (who are slyly watching them), and laugh—"Can you *believe* it?"— to one another at the play's outrageousness. Middle-class Negroes in the audience seem to respond no more honestly than whites, though the presence of *mixed* couples so disturbs other spectators that Jones should perhaps require it in the stage directions.

I concentrate on *The Dutchman* because it is so pure and so effective an example of what I call race-war literature—and, like the work of Larry Rivers (Jones' set designer), so terribly mid-1960's. In a way, the blackness is only symbolic, but then this may be true of the race war itself. The play, one could say, is not really about Negroes at all, except in that only a Negro could have written it—a point that bears thinking on.

Jones—"The Negro James Baldwin"—who is thirty-one, is now founding a Black Theater group in Harlem,

---

* The same may even be true of *Blues for Mister Charlie;* but I really think this is asking too much of a troupe. The text would be fighting their best efforts all the way.

"the big Ghetto," as he calls it, to continue his idea of "Revolutionary Theater"—theater, that is, as revolution. He is collecting money across the country from white liberals, and has gathered a Whitney and a Guggenheim fellowship. He would like, he professes, to incite white audiences to actual violence and black audiences to laughter; but American audiences, as he well knows, are much too cool for that. The warfare will remain for the moment internal and personal, a mind-to-mind combat. In fostering this, he has made a dazzling start. In Los Angeles, not long before the Watts riots, *advertisements* of his plays were banned in the press; his Harlem theater was raided by the police in March 1966 for weapons and dope. Some white people, at least, are taking him seriously.

V
NEGRO WRITERS TODAY:
THE POETS

Few of the poets of the Negro Renaissance, and few of
their themes, any longer hold the stage. For all of Léopold Sédar-Senghor's appeals to *négritude*,* the Afri-
can-identify motif so big in the twenties seems just
about played out. With its withdrawal, much of the
race content has gone out of the better poetry of American Negroes. Some of the leading poets are now writing
skillfully out of regions of the mind far too interior to
betray the color of their skins.

Between Langston Hughes, the leading survivor of
the first generation, and Gwendolyn Brooks, the major
"modern" Negro poet (now over fifty years old), at

---

* This term, not easily susceptible of definition, was popularized by
Léopold Sédar-Senghor, poet and now President of the Republic of
Sénégal. It involves an acceptance and affirmation by the Negro of his
elemental "blackness," physical, cultural, and spiritual.

The idea is an essentially African nationalist (or supranationalist)
one, and has a great deal to do with the existential strain of decoloniza-
tion, the ardent efforts of newly independent black Africans to define for
themselves a cultural identity that has nothing to do with Europe. It has
been defined by Sartre as "anti-racist racism," and supposedly makes itself felt in a freer, more emotional, more "Negro" literature.

Although Senghor has insisted that the concept is meaningful to Negro
Americans as well as Africans, few have taken him up. He urges Negro
Americans, for example, to take the great *African* writers for their classics; but Ralph Ellison (in *Shadow and Act*) specifically asserts his right
to the Greek, Latin, and Western European heritage. In an important
confrontation at the First International Congress of Black Writers and
Artists (Paris, 1956), Richard Wright challenged Senghor directly and
denied the relevance of a black African ancestral culture to the American Negro. "I cannot accept Africa because of mere blackness or on trust.
. . . I question the value of that culture in relationship of [to?] our
future. I do not condemn it. But how can we use it?" (*Présence Afri-
caine*, n.s., No. 8-9-10, June-Nov. 1956, p. 68.)

least a dozen others deserve their anthology places, and some mention here. Briskly ticking them off in a few paragraphs may seem small appreciation. But their best poems are worth reading still; they make a rich and estimable collection of surprising variety. "A Moment Please" (1956) by Paul Vesey (Samuel Allen) —who *has* gone African—is a striking and original restatement, a short, contrapuntal, "inside/outside" report of an encounter with traditional race prejudice. Donald Jeffrey Hayes is a popular magazine verse writer with a schoolboy's sense of metrics; but he has turned out some fine, very delicate poems with an ironic simplicity that recalls Emily Dickinson—poems, usually, on the human qualities and habits to which the American Negro makes a special claim: tiredness, loneliness, suffering, quiet sorrow, endurance, despair, the artificial smile. His longer, more ambitious "Appoggiatura" is a poem in anyone's book, and lovely to read. Among the earlier work of Carl Holman (professor, editor, Civil Rights administrator) are some violent Marxist anti-war, anti-capitalist rants, some embarrassingly dated wartime collages, some 1940's-*moderne* abstract expressionism. But he warrants mention most honorably for his newest vein, more direct and less stylish, represented by three poems in Herbert Hill's 1963 collection *Soon, One Morning*, "The Picnic," "Three Brown Girls Singing," and "Mr. Z." All are quietly barbed race-story poems, mildly obvious journalist verse of the sort mastered by several Negro poets.

Two prize-winning Negro poets still practicing, Melvin Tolson and Margaret Walker, represent in their most celebrated works an unfashionable poetic tradi-

81

tion, a tradition one can acknowledge without admiring. Both declaim with Olympian assurance, in dithyrambic, Whitmanesque paragraphs, long catalogues of Negro social history. In long-breathed stanza lines, they unroll the sufferings (Walker) and achievements (Tolson) of the race. Both speak proudly, or claim to speak, for "The Negro," with a sort of Archibald MacLeishy gusto. If it seems embarrassingly inflated today, the manner doubtless had its justice and its effect in the forties. The two poems most celebrated in Negro circles (Tolson's "Dark Symphony," 1944, and Walker's "For My People," 1942) are, at their best, eloquent declamations, at their worst valuable period pieces like the heroic WPA murals they recall. Both poets have written other interesting things, but it is apparently difficult to relinquish this rhapsodic style once it is adopted. Tolson offered, in 1953, a centennial *Libretto for the Republic of Liberia* of 770 lines. The book has poetry all over it, but it is so freighted with esoteric allusions as to require seventeen pages of footnotes. Except for Liberian patriots with plenty of time, the rewards of reading will probably seem incommensurate with the effort. *Harlem Gallery* (1965), a 170-page opus in the same arcane manner, I found similarly tedious, similarly clogged with literary allusions. In a recent interview, Tolson revealed the source of his strange difficulties.

I had read and absorbed the techniques of Eliot, Pound, Yeats, Baudelaire, Pasternak, and, I believe, all the great Moderns. God only knows how many "little magazines" I studied, and how much textual analysis of the New Critics. . . . the *Li-*

82

bretto is very literary, to say the least. I thought the Establishment, the Academy, would like it.*

Owen Dodson, a Howard University professor, is an author who is *almost* doing several great things, is almost a very important writer, of fiction and drama as well as poetry. His *Powerful Long Ladder* (1946) was full of badly aging propaganda poetry, incantations all capital letters and exclamation points, occasion poetry, too obvious race poetry. But it also included "Lament," a strongly ironic comment on a lynching; "Black Mother Praying," a moving sample of the hopeless Negro prayer; "Engagement," a neat bit of Congrevian wit; "Drunken Lover," powerfully real; and some ineffective ghostly verse dramas blessed by excellent lines. A new volume of poems is due out, as well as a new novel: His day may be at hand.

The two finest poems by Negroes (not the two finest Negro poets) both draw their subjects from the epic history of Negro suffering: Richard Wright's "Between the World and Me," which celebrates an imagined lynching; and Robert Hayden's "Middle Passage," which tells the story of the slave ships and their black cargoes. They have, in the literature of the race war, positions analogous to *Invisible Man* among the novels and *The Dutchman* among the plays. The effect they produce is irresistible and entire, the hurt they give is lasting. It inheres in part, this pain, in the very hell of their subjects, in each case so completely evoked. The effect is certified, though, by the satisfying, spher-

---

* *Anger, and Beyond,* ed. Herbert Hill (Harper and Row, 1966).

83

ical fullness of the design, the exactness of the craft.

Both are long poems, in which one could scarcely change a word with any hope of increasing the rightness or the power. Both are bloody, graphic, even documentary in their detailing of the horror; but so certain and controlled one can *use* the torment. The urge to quote in both cases is irresistible, and appropriate; nothing less than extensive quotation, in the case of Hayden's piece, could acknowledge the brim-full rightness, the necessary alternation of mode and effect.

". . . Some try to starve themselves.
Lost three this morning leaped with crazy laughter
to the waiting sharks, sang as they went under."

   . . . Deep in the festering hold thy father lies,
of his bones New England pews are made,
those are altar lights that were his eyes.

Jesus Savior Pilot Me
Over Life's Tempestuous Sea . . .

". . . Which one of us
has killed an albatross? A plague among
our blacks—Opthalmia: blindness—& we
have jettisoned the blind to no avail.
It spreads, the terrifying sickness spreads.
Its claws have scratched sight from the Capt.'s eyes
& there is blindness in the fo'c'sle
& we must sail 3 weeks before we come
to port."

   What port awaits us, Davy Jones'
or home? I've heard of slavers drifting, drifting,

playthings of wind and storm and chance, their crews
gone blind, the jungle hatred
crawling up on deck.

Thou   Who   Walked   On   Gaililee.

"Deponent further sayeth *The Bella J*
left the Guinea Coast
with cargo of five hundred blacks and odd
for the barracoons of Florida:
"That there was hardly room 'tween-decks for half
the sweltering cattle stowed spoon-fashion there;
that some went mad of thirst and tore their flesh
and sucked the blood:
"That Crew and Captain lusted with the come-liest
of the savage girls kept naked in the cabins;
that there was one they called The Guinea Rose
and they cast lots and fought to lie with her:
"That when the Bo's'n piped all hands, the flames
spreading from starboard already were beyond
control, the Negroes howling and their chains
entangled with the flames:
"That the burning blacks could not be reached,
that the Crew abandoned ship,
leaving their shrieking Negresses behind,
that the Captain perished drunken with the wenches:
"Further Deponent sayeth not."

Pilot   Oh   Pilot   Me . . .

. . . A charnel stench, effluvium of living death
spreads outward from the hold,
where the living and the dead, the horribly
　　dying,
lie interlocked, lie foul with blood and excre-
ment.
　　Deep in the festering hold thy father lies,
　　the corpse of mercy rots with him,
　　rats eat love's rotten gelid eyes.
　　But, oh, the living look at you
　　with human eyes whose suffering accuses
　　　　you,
　　whose hatred reaches through the swill of
　　　　dark
　　to strike you like a leper's claw.
　　You cannot stare that hatred down
　　or chain the fear that stalks the watches
　　and breathes on you its fetid scorching
　　　　breath;
　　cannot kill the deep immortal human wish,
　　the timeless will. . . .

Hayden, a "major" Negro poet, has written many other
poems, professional and stylish: Communist and Afri-
can-memory poems, war poems, Negro hero poems,
poems overfilled with a sort of decadent delirious excess of hallucinatory imagery. But it all now seems, in
unfair retrospect, apprentice work for "Middle Passage."

Wright's poem, "Between the World and Me,"
forms a perfect-circle experience, from objective suggestion to imagination to experience, and then back to
the dead object of suggestion. None of the many torture

sequences in his stories or novels has anything like the effect of this poem. Never was his notorious intensity so controlled.

And one morning while in the woods I stumbled suddenly upon the thing,
Stumbled upon it in a grassy clearing guarded
by scaly oaks and elms.
And the sooty details of the scene rose, thrusting themselves between the world and
me. . . .

There was a design of white bones slumber-
ing forgottenly upon a cushion of ashes.
There was a charred stump of a sapling point-
ing a blunt finger accusingly at the sky.
There were torn tree limbs, tiny veins of
burnt leaves, and a scorched coil of greasy
hemp;
A vacant shoe, an empty tie, a ripped shirt, a
lonely hat, and a pair of trousers stiff with
black blood.
And upon the trampled grass were buttons,
dead matches, butt-ends of cigars and cigarettes, peanut shells, a drained gin-flask,
and a whore's lipstick;
Scattered traces of tar, restless arrays of
feathers, and the lingering smell of gasoline.
And through the morning air the sun poured
yellow surprise into the eye sockets of a
stony skull. . . .
And while I stood my mind was frozen with
a cold pity for the life that was gone.

The ground gripped my feet and my heart
was circled by icy walls of fear—

The sun died in the sky; a night wind mut-
tered in the grass and fumbled the leaves
in the trees; the woods poured forth the
hungry yelping of hounds; the darkness
screamed with thirsty voices; and the wit-
nesses rose and lived:

The dry bones stirred, rattled, lifted, melting
themselves into my bones.

The grey ashes formed flesh firm and black,
entering into my flesh.

The gin-flask passed from mouth to mouth;
cigars and cigarettes glowed, the whore
smeared the lipstick red upon her lips,

And a thousand faces swirled around me,
clamoring that my life be burned. . . .

And then they had me, stripped me, batter-
ing my teeth into my throat till I swal-
lowed my own blood.

My voice was drowned in the roar of their
voices, and my black wet body slipped and
rolled in their hands as they bound me to
the sapling.

And my skin clung to the bubbling hot tar,
falling from me in limp patches.

And the down and quills of the white feathers
sank into my raw flesh, and I moaned in
my agony.

Then my blood was cooled mercifully, cooled
by a baptism of gasoline.

And in a blaze of red I leaped to the sky as
  pain rose like water, boiling my limbs.
Panting, begging I clutched childlike,
  clutched to the hot sides of death.
Now I am dry bones and my face a stony
  skull staring in yellow surprise at the
  sun. . . .

Gwendolyn Brooks, who won the Pulitzer Prize for
poetry in 1950, is a writer of an entirely different order
from any of these. She is, in the context of this survey,
far more a poet than a Negro; for she is totally a poet,
totally dedicated to her craft. She exercises, customarily, a greater degree of artistic control than any other
American Negro writer. Not even Ralph Ellison has
attained her level of objective and exquisite detachment. At least one Negro, it is worth noting, in the
postwar United States, a Chicago mother and teacher,
has been able to transcend the assertedly "universal"
plight of her race. She is no more professionally black
than T. S. Eliot (whose manner and skills she recalls),
and should really be read and judged in the colorless
company of his followers.

Of all Negro practitioners, only LeRoi Jones demands the same degree of poetic respect as Gwendolyn
Brooks. They share a seriousness of poetic purpose,
an intensely modern idiom (as opposed to Langston
Hughes' "timelessness"), and a coterie audience (as
opposed to his popularity). But Jones is a beatific,
Blakean disbeliever in words, thrashing out raw problems of self-definition and epistemological truth in hopeless, anti-verbal expressions, all pain and incoherence.
For Gwendolyn Brooks, at the other extreme, the is-

sues, the self have all been sublimated into problems of craft, problems which she precisely and coolly solves.

What she seems to have done is to have chosen, as her handle on the "real" (often the horribly real), the other reality of craftsmanship, of technique. With this she has created a highly stylized screen of imagery and diction and sound—fastidiously exact images, crisp Mandarin diction, ice-perfect sound—to stand between the reader and the subject; to stand often so glittering and sure that all he can ever focus on is the screen. The "subjects"—racial discrimination, mother love, suffering—are dehumanized into *manerismo* figurines, dancing her meters. It is *her* intelligence, *her* imagination, *her* brilliant wit and wordplay that entrap the attention. Always, the subjects are held at arm's length away. Whoever the persona—and she is often forced to make the speakers fastidious, alienated creatures like herself—it is always her mind and her style we are dwelling in.

This can (to a reader still concerned with "subjects") run to excess, when all "idea" is honed away in overcontrol, when all that is left, it seems, is wordplay and allusion and technique: crisp, brisk phrases and images like the taps of steel spike heels, going nowhere. In many of her early poems (especially the *Annie Allen* poems) Mrs. Brooks appears only to pretend to talk of things and of people; her real love is words. The inlay work of words, the *précieux* sonics, the lapidary insets of jeweled images (like those of Gerard Manley Hopkins) can, in excess, squeeze out life and impact altogether, and all but give the lie to the passions professed in the verbs.

The style itself cannot be described briefly. There is enough new-bought diction and shivery tonic phrasing and rhythmic play to fascinate a university seminar in modern poetics for months. She has learned her art superbly. The words, lines, and arrangements have been worked and worked and worked again into poised exactness: the unexpected apt metaphor, the mock-colloquial asides amid jeweled phrases, the half-ironic repetitions—she knows it all. The stylistic critic could only, at his most keen, fault the rare missed stitch of accent, the off-semitone of allusion.

Where, in all of this, is Gwendolyn Brooks? Anywhere? In the proper Donne-to-Eliot manner, she objectifies herself, for the most part, into the figured screen, her "blackness" becomes part of its peacocky color. She is become "all tone," all voice, all fire and air. One can only intuit the inspiring impulses of her works from the intensity of their objective design.

This is not to say she never speaks directly, or communicates ideas—even race-war ideas. There *are* clear direct statements, human portraits, in *A Street in Bronzeville* (1945)—though even in the best ("The Mother," for example) technical overcontrol may prevent the full realization of potential power (a matter of fear?). *Annie Allen* (1950), the Pulitzer Prize volume, is the most Mandarin; but sections VIII and especially XV of "The Womanhood" sequence bring a seething racial intensity of statement that for once gives the controlling art something to control, and produces genuine emotional tension. The latter may be the best statement yet on the latent Jim Crowism of white liberal society, a donation by a real artist to the Negro War Fund.

91

Men of careful turns, haters of forks in the
road,
The strain at the eye, that puzzlement, that
awe—
Grant me that I am human, that I hurt,
That I can cry.

Not that I now ask alms, in shame gone hollow,
Nor cringe outside the loud and sumptuous
gate.
Admit me to our mutual estate.

Open my rooms, let in the light and air.
Reserve my service at the human feast.
And let the joy continue. Do not hoard silence
For the moment when I enter, tardily,
To enjoy my height among you. And to love
you
No more as a woman loves a drunken mate,
Restraining full caress and good My Dear,
Even pity for the heaviness and the need—
Fearing sudden fire out of the uncaring
mouth,
Boiling in the slack eyes, and the traditional
blow.
Next, the indifference formal, deep and slow.
Comes in your graceful glider and benign,
To smile upon me bigly; now desires
Me easy, easy; claims the days are softer
Than they were; murmurs reflectively "Re-
member

When cruelty, metal, public, uncomplex,
Trampled you obviously and every hour . . ."
(Now cruelty flaunts diplomas, is elite,
Delicate, has polish, knows how to be dis-
    creet):
    Requests my patience, wills me to be calm,
    Brings me a chair, but the one with broken
        straw,
    Whispers "My friend, no thing is without
        flaw,
    If prejudice is native—and it is—you
    Will find it ineradicable—not to
    Be juggled, not to be altered at all,
    But left unvexed at its place in the proper-
        ness
    Of things, even to be given (with grudg-
        ing) honor.
    What
    We are to hope is that intelligence
    Can sugar up our prejudice with polite-
        ness.
    Politeness will take care of what needs
        caring.
    For the line is there.
    And has a meaning. So our fathers said—
    And they were wise—we think—At any
        rate,
    They were older than ourselves. And the
        report is
    What's old is wise. At any rate, the line is
    Long and electric. Lean beyond and nod.
    Be sprightly. Wave. Extend your hand and
        teeth.

But never forget it stretches there be-
neath."
The toys are all grotesque
And not for lovely hands; are dangerous,
Serrate in open and artful places. Rise.
Let us combine. There are no magics or elves
Or timely godmothers to guide us. We are
lost, must
Wizard a track through our own screaming
need.

The same is true, somewhat less deeply, of "Lovers of
the Poor" from *The Bean Eaters* (1959), a suave attack
on overcultured whites by one who understands overcul-
ture, who can treasure herself the riches she mocks.
Elsewhere in this latest book Mrs. Brooks tries to expand
her human scale—there are a few poignant husband-
wife portraits in the manner of her novella *Maud
Martha*, even attempts at jazz. But her fine efforts to
take arms (an Emmett Till poem, a Little Rock poem,
poems on white snobbery and neighborhood-mixing
themes) betray the author through their tissues of arcane allusion, their perfectly chopped metrics. Gwendolyn Brooks has too little of the common touch to be
of much use in the war; but she offers, through her
painstaking, exquisite art, the example of one woman
who has come through.

Of the most recent generation of poets, all I know is
what I have read in the anthologies (*American Negro
Poetry*, edited by Arna Bontemps, 1963, and *New Negro
Poets USA*, edited by Langston Hughes, 1964), and the
work of LeRoi Jones. The small Hughes-edited volume

is for the most part a collection of lifeless academic poetry (Fisk, Howard, Atlanta, Lincoln, the New Negro college crowd), with a few Beats thrown in for good measure. It is no better or worse, I suppose, than the standard of 1964 poetry. One wonders, sometimes, how poetry editors pick one piece over another; or if anyone other than the author is ever tempted to read such things over twice. The best new poems in the collections seem to me to be those of LeRoi Jones (in a moment); Margaret Danner's "Far from Africa," a chaste, crafted piece of introspection, full of aristocratic rhythms and real things; Dudley Randall's "Southern Road," a sophisticated rendering of the return-to-the-South theme; and Mari Evans' brash little quick-lined slaps like "The Rebel" or "And the Old Women Gathered."

> and the old women gathered
> and sang His praises
> standing
> resolutely together
> like supply sergeants who
> have seen
> everything
> and are still
> Regular Army: It
> was fierce and
> not melodic and
> although we ran
> the sound of it
> stayed in our ears . . .

Ted Joans is the family Beat (there are a few others), self-indulging in the usual hipster way. "The .38" is a stunning existential happening poem of his, a tattoo of forty or fifty lines each beginning "I hear," describing from inside what it is like to be shot to death. A number of good poets contribute clear, slightly old-fashioned anthology pieces on The Race. And Horace Julian Bond, representing the very latest generation (born in 1940, he was a student sit-in leader, a director of SNCC, and was elected in 1965 to the Georgia legislature), made a good pop start with "The Bishop of Atlanta: Ray Charles"; though he is likely to be identified for a while, at least, with his classic couplet on the Civil Rights movement,

> Look at that gal shake that thing—
> We can't all be Martin Luther King.

LeRoi Jones has published (in addition to his plays) two volumes of poetry, *Preface to a Twenty-Volume Suicide Note* (1961) and *The Dead Lecturer* (1964), and an expressionistic, semi-autobiographical, semi-pornographic prose thing called *The System of Dante's Hell* (1965). He is the most difficult of all the Negro poets, and it is hard to say whether any reader can be guaranteed a just repayment for his efforts. It is hard, in fact, to say anything sensible or useful about a poet, who is himself not simply irrational but anti-rational; whose whole approach to poetic language reaches far beyond mere coherence or what we would call sense; who is highly suspicious of the whole nature of verbal communication. This may be one of those many occasions when the wise critic would simply shut up.

> A compromise
> would be silence. To shut up, even such risk
> as the proper placement

of verbs and nouns. To freeze the spit
in mid-air, as it aims itself
at some valiant intellectual's face.

But to give an idea, not to judge, not to interpret:
There is, first, a small group of poems that work very
nearly in the manner of ordinary sense (at least for a
poet). The title poem and "The Turncoat" from the first
volume, "Duncan Spoke of a Process," "If Into Love
The Image Burdens," "I Substitute For The Dead Lecturer," "Snake Eyes," perhaps "Footnote To A Pretentious Book," and especially "The Liar" from the second
volume: these are all quiet, poignantly quiet pieces of
introspection, honest and painful, suggestive, intimate,
coolly sad: Jones on Jones. They reveal, even in their
own moody illogic, a man who wants very much to know
who he is, and wants the reader to know and love him
too. These are inside poems, straight from the pain.

I want to be sung. I want
all my bones and meat hummed
against the thick floating
winter sky. I want myself
as dance. . . .
And let me once, create
myself. And let you, whoever
sits now breathing on my words
create a self of your own. One
that will love me.

I am what I think I am. You are what
I think you are. The world is the
one thing, that will not move. It is
made of stone, round, and very ugly.

97

> Though I am a man
> who is loud
> on the birth
> of his ways. Publicly redefining
> each change in my soul, as if I had predicted
> them . . .
>   When they say, "It is Roi
> who is dead?" I wonder
> who will they mean?

This much is anyone's. One familiar with Jones' plays, too, will catch, here and there, the violent racist anger, particularly in the two strong anti-syntactic "speeches," in "Black Dada Nihilismus," a Kill-All-the-Whites manifesto in dada, and in the surrealist abuse of "Rhythm and Blues" and "Green Lantern's Solo," two of his strongest poems. The violence here is a kind of nightmare violence, something one puts together out of frightening fragments. The two latter poems (from *The Dead Lecturer*) may be as close to a testament as Jones will ever offer, if one knew where to find it; the most honest possible expression of a man who simply cannot trust words to stay still.

> I am deaf and blind and lost and will not again
>   sing your quiet verse. I have lost
> even the act of poetry, and writhe now for
>   cool horizonless dawn . . .

More frequently, the communication is nowhere so definable. It is a nonverbal communication that uses words and phrases only as little pressures on the reader's consciousness, a communication that has very little to

98

do with normal syntax or denotative structure. One reads, at best, a tone. The *Suicide Note* poems ("early LeRoi Jones"?) like "Hymn for Lanie Poo" have a brash, jazzy, young man's sound—a lot of pop-art black humor, jerky collages à la Rauschenberg of radio serial heroes or comic-strip characters taken seriously. As he admits,

> These words
> are not music. They make no motions
> for a dance.

One is denied even the surface attractions of rhythm, except for a jarring sort of skittery jerkiness, or occasional cool riffs on a theme; the "From an Almanac" poems come nearest to modern jazz. Otherwise, the reader must be content to rest passive, to float along with the unresolved surrealistic progress, as Jones plays about with his parentheses and camp gags and insets of sense in search of a style.

The Dead Lecturer poems are even sparer of sense, less attractive, more steely chill, devoid of even the comic gamey glibness of the earlier Jones. But they are even harder to reject absolutely. We have more odd noodling about with word noises, pages in which no single word group between periods coheres into sense. "Obscure" is too concrete a word: lists, insults, four-letter words, parentheses that don't close, lost commas, cold cuts of sound, allusions, dim suggestions of sex or of characters (there are two hazy "character" sequences, on Crow Jane and Willie Best) blend about in the half light, the murky background of dissonance, not nonsense but not sense. For lines and lines the words may lie positively dead, say nothing at all. Then out of it all leap sudden glints and rills of image or statement or pain, three words, a paragraph, a page. This happens especially in the abstract-expressionist protest poems like "Rhythm and Blues"; the evocative and *crafted* poems full of keen dreams and emergent pain: "A Contract," "The Politics of Rich Painters," all lethal and queerly vivid things. Here, in his non-sense, he attacks with surrealist vigor all the common muck that passes for sense.

It is all, ultimately, anti-rational poetry, an attempt at a new stimulation of consciousness through words made malleable. Jones of course is not the only one practicing it, and his identification with Beat poets like Duncan, Olson, and Snyder is appropriate. Rational criticism is unequipped, in the last analysis, to deal with such an effort, and finally irrelevant. It is poetry for the leisured, the patient, the energetic, for those who do not insist on an immediate show of gain for energies expended.

VI
NEGRO WRITERS TODAY:
THE NOVELISTS I

It is to the novel that the new writer today most naturally turns, particularly if he is a new writer of unso-
phisticated origins, with serious problems, a serious
cause, and a need to be heard. For example, an American
Negro. He is allowed, in a novel, the directness and
release of an autobiography (without the embarrass-
ment), the opinionated outspokenness of an essay: and
all the room he wants for self-indulgent, self-satisfying
fiction—fantasies of escape, of revenge, of self-abase-
ment, of social or sensual gratification. It is the freest,
least bounded of forms, with the fewest rules, a home
for the artful and the artless; and (in case of success)
the most popular; the most lucrative. It has been the
form most notably and commonly adopted for the imaginative verbal expression of American Negroes in
recent years.

There have been somewhat over a hundred novels or
collections of stories by Negroes published in the United
States since Richard Wright's *Native Son* (1940), the
first Negro fiction to have endured much beyond its own
season—out of a total by all Americans during this period of perhaps twenty thousand. I have read, or tried to
read, about half of these. These books form the great
bulk of American Negro literature—nine-tenths, at
least, of the lot. It is to the novels one is usually referring
in discussing it (three book-length critical studies have
been published already on the Negro novel) and it is

to these novels I will devote the largest part of this discussion. Our four playwrights, our dozen or so poets have produced varied, imaginative, and effective work; they can teach the outsider a great deal about the "experience of being Negro," and the best of their work is at least equal to the best of the novelists'. But the very freedom, the looseness and openness of the fictional form have kept it the primary receptacle for Negro writers' recollections and dreams, their warnings and threats and hidden fears. So, conversely, does it remain a white reader's surest way to discover (the first-hand sources being presumed impenetrable) what it is like to live in a Negro head, in a Negro home, in a Negro ghetto.

A discussion of the American Negro novel focuses on three leading figures: Richard Wright, Ralph Ellison, and James Baldwin. These are three very large men, painfully different and independent, each sick and atypical in his own American way.

WRIGHT

Richard Wright is a figure of almost primeval simplicity. There is something about him of the fundamentalist, the Old Testament prophet. His imagination was seized by the race-war myth in its starkest, most unsubtle forms. There is almost nothing in his fiction of tenderness or ambiguity. He is gigantic, unlovable, unequivocal, humorless and artless, monolithic; and necessary. His voice was and is a *necessary* voice, crude and unpleasant like a siren.

He was a man far simpler than his two great successors of the fifties and sixties, undivided by their ambivalent sympathies, their trying sense of contingency.

His ready adoption of communism (which dates his fiction more than anything else, in this unideological age) evinces this moral simplicity: he seems an earlier variety of man. He was confident of his own righteousness, and that of his black-and-white moral mythology. The white men in his stories are usually flat figures of undetailed evil—which is all they can be, in the terms of his myth. Their deaths, like their motives, simply do not matter. His amoralist Negro heroes, on the other hand, can become tormented martyrs. The only possible relationship, in his scheme, is hate; the only significant action is murder. Out of this austere mythology, Wright created a number of bludgeoning bloody tales with cleaver-cut plots, true more in their awful total effect than in any of their details.

Such a view of Wright, of Wright seen through his fiction, is borne out by the almost autobiographical *Black Boy* of 1945. This book, the most outspoken of all Negro protest autobiographies, is a necessary document in the race warrior's kit, along with the classic essay which prefigured it, "The Ethics of Living Jim Crow" (1937). These two works clearly set forth for the first time the inside dimension of the Negro's experience of prejudice in America: what it feels like to live in the mad prison house of sadistic white obsessions. In them was detailed, for perhaps the first time, the Negro's whole elaborate ritual of survival. For this alone, they are as important as anything Wright (or any American Negro) has written.

But *Black Boy* also reveals its author-hero (never was author more heroic) as a man governed by the most absolute, unreflective, and uncritical certitude of his own virtue. He has had, it would seem, no mean or ignoble motives, no mixed motives even. Any "faults" that appear in the boy Richard are the result of others' moral blindness. He possessed, from infancy nearly, a humorless ethical monumentality; the world is a moral arena for the young Prince Arthur-Wright. Every episode is seen as another fierce combat in the career of this militant young atheist martyr.

In a way—under the rules of his racial-moral myth—he is right. As the oppressed, unregarded American scapegoat, he *can* regard himself as a vessel of righteousness; he has the right. What this implies, though, is that Wright was never able to see himself, or other men, or the Negro Problem, or anything else (see his view of world history in *White Man, Listen!*) except in the shape of the fixed abstractions of his moral myth.

His fictions, then, follow naturally from his character and his vision. They are—to oversimplify—usually epic dramatizations of the race war at its most intense: lynching, murder, fire, beating, castration, psychotic sex combats, police brutality, race riots, pure hate against pure hate. His backgrounds (notoriously in *Native Son*) are vivid displays of sullen Negro slum life, his characters symbolic racial antagonists of an epic, sometimes existential simplicity. His Negroes, however "wicked," are always morally victorious in defeat. In an extended example like *The Long Dream*, he will use one Negro's story as an exemplary biography of racial oppression—the standard pattern for the protest novel. He may descend (as in Max's speech in *Native Son*) to explicit moral justification of his myth. Communism frequently plays a part, more often as party than as dogma, even after Wright's disaffection in 1950. (He was one of the contributors to *The God That Failed*.)

104

The most affecting element of his fictions, however, is likely to be the brutal detailing of horror that is very nearly his trademark. No one describes a lynching, a burning, a dismembering with quite the same evident gusto.* It is this, as often as not, that provides the raw material behind Wright's explosions: a girl's head is sawn off in order to fit her body into a furnace; still sizzling black corpses are dragged out of a burning dance hall; a dog is slowly eviscerated with a knife; a little boy's body makes a "cushy PLOP!" on the sidewalk after a ten-story fall. The effect of such horrors, such subliterary sadism, is perhaps no more "useful," socially, no more legitimate or lasting than that of the pornography it resembles. The offense may have been intentional; or the expressions may have simply been essential to Wright's sanity. (James Baldwin thinks they are there "in place of sex.") But no reader of Wright is likely to be able to avoid or forget them.

The stories of *Uncle Tom's Children*, predating *Native Son*, have about them an early American directness, a hard New England austerity. Moral issues were never again, for Wright, to be of such Homeric simplicity; his black heroes never again so heroically right, his white men never such a dehumanized mob of evil. The finest story, "Down by the Riverside," depicts the barren, Job-like sufferings and destruction of a black man and his family during a tempestuous flood, which carries the reader in its force. In the course of his agonies, the Negro shoots and kills a white man, which is of course

---

* Verbal sadism (or masochism), in the guise of white anti-Negro insults, is closely related to this: "Every decent white man in America ought to swoon with joy for the opportunity to crush with his heel the woolly head of this black lizard, to keep him from scuttling on his belly farther over the earth and spitting forth his venom of death!" says the prosecutor in *Native Son*.

necessary and right. It is only *his* death at the end, when he is shot down for the murder, that is made to seem tragic, and wasteful, and wrong.

Native Son, and especially its hero Bigger Thomas, has been a storm center of acrimonious racial-literary controversy for twenty-five years. By now it may perhaps be granted that Bigger is not only atypical but incredible: no one quite like him ever was or will be. The communist ideology may be skimmed off as something curdled by age, something gray and inessential. The asserted morality (*Nous [blancs] sommes tous des assassins*) and the Sartrean philosophy may be granted their measure of mythic, not documentary, truth. The novel may be acknowledged, moreover, as one of the most artless, ineffably crude efforts of Dreiserian naturalism—artless and crude both in design and in texture —in American fiction. All this, I think, may be granted, and *Native Son* still keep its place. Time does wonderful things.

What remain are a vivid portrait of the Chicago ghetto, the pathos of Bessie (Bigger's girl) and Bigger's mother, and especially the searing indictment of an American populace in heat. White America, as reflected during the hunt-turned-pogrom, in the streets, in the press, at the trial, is offered a convincing and usable reflection of its lowest self.

The real value of the book—and this applies to all of Wright's fiction—lies not in the simplistic and too easily resistible moral lessons he purposely implants, but rather in the quite different moral "lesson," moral activity the reader may extract. What this will be I cannot say; it will differ for each reader. It is *not*, or it should not be a simple-minded bowing of white heads before

106

the black racist lash. In the words of Bigger's lawyer, at the trial,

> The very concept of injustice rests upon a premise of equal claims, and this boy here today makes no claim upon you. If you think or feel that he does, then you, too, are blinded by a feeling as terrible as that which you condemn in him, and without as much justification. The feeling of guilt which has caused all of the mob-fear and mob-hysteria is the counterpart of his own hate.

Any *simple* response to the book is a lie. The moral issues permit neither gulping total acceptance (if this were possible) nor indignant total rejection—not even on the grounds of art.

Most of the obvious, spontaneous responses, in fact, are secondary, and should be transcended. The book is intended as a weapon, and it can be used as a test. It *will* arouse, excite, inflame; the double murders, the visceral tensions and horrors, all the "unbearable" qualities cannot help but be offensive. The imperious moral claims are bound to intimidate and bewilder. But one can *use* an exacerbated imagination, a critical vertigo, a moral sense unanchored and set spinning. One can use these books, and their unpleasant effects, as a moral probe of himself. For there is, back of it all, back of the sadistic racist-moralist bullying, a mountainous justice in Wright's fictional claims, and he cannot be entirely denied. *Native Son* remains, in all senses, an awful book.

After this first novel, in the years of his exile (one's image of Wright in Paris, unfortunately, is perverted by James Baldwin's acutely nasty memoir, "Alas, Poor Richard"), Wright's fiction lost much of its force. *The*

Long Dream (1958) is a useful book, as good as many Negroes' novels. It has its own violence, its potency, its gut-effectiveness, its convincing detail; but the whole is too artless to be emotionally credible. It wants the simple mythic surety of the first book. *The Outsider* (1953) is a flat, windy rewriting of *Native Son:* an angry sadist seems to be flogging his dead imagination. *Eight Men* (1961, posthumously published), a collection of short stories, was an attempt to recapture the simple intensities of *Uncle Tom's Children;* in a few instances—"The Man Who Saw the Flood," "The Man Who Was Almost a Man," "The Man Who Killed a Shadow"—it succeeds. But much of the rest is too consciously contrived, "arty" without being art. "The Man Who Lived Underground," from the collection, was Wright's most determined attempt to prove himself an artist, an objective, symbolist craftsman like Ralph Ellison. It has, one must grant, all the materials of an impressive tale; but it wants the sense of style, of arrangement, of finish and *mesure*. Wright was not and would never be an "artist"; his lecture (in *White Man, Listen!*) on American Negro literature demonstrates his tin ear for style.

After *Eight Men* all we have are some fragments of a novel (apparently a continuation of *The Long Dream*, set in Paris) in the Hill anthology *Soon, One Morning*, a parody of his earlier self. The café celebrity was now epochs away from the race war that had given him his literary *raison d'être*, all genuine passion spent. He died in 1960.

As both Ellison and Baldwin have made clear, Wright is not, in any sense, a representative American Negro. His militant anti-religious atheism (from the age

108

of—what? ten?), his alienation from family and community, his sincere claim that there is "a strange absence of any real kindness in Negroes," or of honor, loyalty, tenderness, love—all of this contrasts markedly not only with the experience of a Baldwin, say, for he is not "typical" either—but with that, I am sure—of most other living American Negroes. Wright himself confessed (in *Black Boy*) the distance he felt from other Negroes. He marveled at their laughter, their resilience, their so easy adaptation to "a separate, stunted way of life," when all he was ever able to do was resist and fight back. He may never have come to understand white men; but he never understood many Negroes, either.

His own mythic dramatization of the Negro as a pure engine of hate, brutalized, behavioristic, driven by unrelieved suffering ("Multiply Bigger Thomas twelve million times . . . and you have the psychology of the Negro people") is as stultifying and incomplete a stereotype (as Ellison and Baldwin have agreed) as any white Southerner's "nigger." Like most useful myths, it is in great part false, but this does not make it any less useful.

And the same applies to Richard Wright, for all his once-in-twelve-million uniqueness—a man in great part "false," atypical, exceptional, but no less useful for that.

> An infant crying in the night,
> An infant crying for the light,
> And with no language but a cry.

He, after all, was real. If he was not telling all the truth, neither was he lying. The fact that he was obsessed, as a writer, with sadism and brutality grants us no permission to ignore the fact that there *is*, in white America's treatment of the Negro, a great deal of sadism and brutality. If white America did not make Bigger Thomas, as his lawyer insisted it did—and let us not be too sure —it *did* make Richard Wright, for whom Bigger Thomas was necessary.

ELLISON

Ralph (Waldo) Ellison stands at the opposite end of the writer's world from Richard Wright. Although he is as aware of the issues of the race war as anyone else, he is no more a consciously active participant than, say, Gwendolyn Brooks or William Faulkner. "I wasn't, and am not, primarily concerned with injustice, but with art." He achieves his extraordinary power through artistry and control, through objectivity, irony, distance: he works with symbol rather than with act. He is at least as much an artist as a Negro. He accepts both roles so naturally, in fact, that he has made them one. His one novel, the supreme work of art created by an American Negro, is essentially a Negro's novel. It is written entirely out of a Negro's experience, and reveals its full dimension, I am convinced, only to the perfect *Negro* reader. But it is not a "Negro novel." Like Gwendolyn Brooks, like Faulkner, like most serious artists, he has transmuted himself and his experience almost entirely into his art. Only by turning to his essays and interviews can one discover the degree to which his own opinions, on racial issues or any other, are implicit in *Invisible Man.*

Invisible Man (1952) was not, Ellison insists, "an attack upon white society." The fact that so many white readers saw it as such says interesting things about white readers—so ridden with guilt they cannot wait

110

for a Negro to accuse them. It is not, really, a race-war novel. But as no Negro's life in America, not even in the symbolic recreation, can be entirely free of racial combat, there are elements in the book that can be legitimately read in a race-war context.

Since the story is primarily that of the growth into awareness of the nameless colored hero, many of the steps in his growth involve lessons in racial realism, the rules for survival in a white man's world, "the ethics of living Jim Crow." His sage old grandfather enjoins him, on his deathbed (the first page of the first chapter), to "Overcome 'em with yeses, undermine 'em with grins, agree 'em to death and destruction"—which might be taken as a basic Negro code in the etiquette of war. His greatest leap into awareness later on, his most jarring disillusionment, comes in the confessional abuse of Dr. Bledsoe:

> ". . . haven't we bowed and scraped and begged and lied enough decent homes and drives for you to show him? . . .
>
> "Ordered you?" he said. "He *ordered* you. Dammit, white folk are always giving orders, it's a habit with them. . . . My God, boy! You're black and living in the South—did you forget how to lie? . . . Why, the dumbest black bastard in the cotton patch knows that the only way to please a white man is to tell him a lie! . . ."

Later one encounters ironic portrayals of white liberal confusion, of the hero's desperate attempts not to act like a Southern Negro—other parts of the elaborate rite.

Several instances of direct propaganda occur, although each time in so organically convincing a situation that one does not think of attributing them to Ellison directly. They are simply taken as true, dramatically and substantially. Most notable are the harangue of the mad Negro doctor at the Golden Day (Chapter 3)—it is a distinctly "Ellison" touch to make the truth-teller mad; and the hero's superbly moving funeral oration in Chapter 21, "His Name was Clifton." By Chapter 21, even he can tell the truth. "His name was Clifton and he was black and they shot him down."

". . . Such was the short bitter life of Brother Tod Clifton. Now he's in this box with the bolts tightened down. He's in the box and we're in there with him, and when I've told you this you can go. It's dark in this box and it's crowded. It has a cracked ceiling and a clogged-up toilet in the hall. It has rats and roaches and it's far, far too expensive a dwelling. The air is bad and it'll be cold this winter. Tod Clifton is crowded and he needs the room. 'Tell them to get out of the box,' that's what he would say if you could hear him. . . ."

The political plot, the Brotherhood story of the second half of the novel is itself turned, by author and actors, to racial purpose. It is not the very fire of the novel, the creative or significant center: the hero's mind is that. But it takes up so much of his, the author's, and the reader's concerns during the second 250 pages that it acquires nearly independent status. And its primary issue is the battle between the Black Nationalists of Ras the Destroyer (= "race") and the interracial Brotherhood for the dominion of Harlem. When the Brotherhood appears to desert the Negro cause, when one of its ex-leaders is shot, a spectacular race riot (which Ellison drew from the Harlem riots of 1943 and 1950) explodes. The Invisible Man is driven underground, and the novel ends. So for half the novel at least, one might well think that race war was the point at issue.

The most substantial, the most original race-war element of the book, however, may be less apparent. Each of the vivid symbolic episodes—the battle royal; the Golden Day; Liberty Paints ("Keep America Pure with Liberty Paints," the most celebrated being their "Optic White"); the forced electric lobotomy; the dispossession of an old Harlem couple—each of these scenes tells more about the race issue than chapters of more explicit commentary or drama could do. Consider the virtually limitless implications of the paint company explosion: Liberty Paints (white) is blown up, presumably destroyed, by an accidental excess of boiler pressure on the (Negro-run) basement valves. It is all, on one level, quite credible; the explicit racial narrative is reasonable and socially realistic. But the *implicit* conflict is as awesome, as gigantic, as it is in the world outside of novels.

It does not take a show of force, though, real or symbolic, to prove that a war is on: the very quality of the Negro's existence in America is proof of that. "Our life is a war," the hero's grandfather tells him, and this book is, among other things, a complete story of Negro life in America. By nature something of a pacifist, a quietist, Ellison is much more free than the embattled protestors like Wright to try to tell *all* of the Negro's story. It has been the theme of his entire creative life, in fact, that there is far, far more to the Negro's story in America than oppression, suffering, and hate: "The view from inside the skin," he insists, "is not so dark as it appears to be."

113

Ellison has managed, with the deftest concision, to write a shorthand history and sociology of the American Negro, in the life and opinions of his prototypical hero. One symbolic instance—the eviction of two aged Harlem Negroes—not only triggers the hero's activist phase (and Part II of the book), but also affords Ellison a chance for the most closely focused review of the Negro's story in America. Among the couple's tattered, scrambled effects, cast out on the street, are artifacts and mementoes from every stage of the American Negro past: minstrel show bones; voodoo nuggets; an Ethiopian flag; a tintype of Lincoln; a picture of a banjo-strumming, blackfaced white man; a yellowing headline of Garvey's deportation; a Hollywood pin-up; a St. Louis Fair plate; and a set of manumission papers, dated August, 1859.

The focus of all this propaganda and history and ironic sociology is the nameless hero, the Invisible Man ("invisible," that is, to white men's eyes), the Negroes' Joseph K. It is his story, really, not the race's, not the war's, except insofar as he is of the race and in the war. (His non-naming, through five hundred pages, never becomes obvious or ominous—a testimony to the subtlety of Ellison's art. It is simply never needed.) The creation and loving sustenance of this narrator-hero, with all his follies and limitations, are among the triumphs of the book.

Reaching out from the central artifice of the narrator-hero are other displays of Ellison's art. His style, the "fine texture," is exact and acute, the language (usually) at fingertip control. Hear the crisp offhandedness of wicked ironies, the cool black humor; or—as in the chapter in Hill's anthology (*Soon, One Morning*)—the needle-sharp evocations of sensation and interior pain. He can manipulate language, as he can character, event, and design, for the optimum effects of irony, of a balanced double vision. Certain devices, tiny tricks, he leaves about like fingerprints: the strange selectivity of detail that leaves characters and objects and events undefinably charged, "off," ever so slightly left of real; the pre-announcement of a thing some lines before it is identified, giving to it an eerie surreality. Ellison has also, to move to items of slightly larger focus, the fullest sense of drama; he knows when to signal and advance a key moment, how to pace and position effects for the fullest build-up of artful tension or comedy or suspense: he can work up cool quiet horror like Harold Pinter, or handle the giant crescendo of effects needed for pageants like Clifton's funeral or the Harlem riots.

His rhetorical skill is prodigious, and he is not reticent about displaying its range. Not only does he indulge himself in perfect mimicry of the tall tale, the emotion-charged address, the Negro sermon; he also allows himself chances for Joycean word display, and makes his hero's hold on history a "way with words," a gift of tongues, an awesome and dangerous eloquence like his own.

Ellison's creative imagination, if such a talent can be singly regarded, is also more prolific than that of his peers. His exotic range of living characters, their vividness and magnitude; the extraordinary sequence of scenes and situations, each rendered with overflowing fullness—rooms, inner states, mob scenes, the fantasia of the hospital, the unforgettable battle royal at the Southern white men's smoker with which the novel opens: such independent creations bear witness to one

115

of the most awesomely fertile living imaginations in American writing.

The book is told, for the most part, in a sequence of vivid scenic blocks, held together by the various threads of continuity: the hero's emerging character, the world's conspiracy to "keep him running," the race history his story encloses. But the greatest force of unity is the common quality of each of these scenic blocks. They possess a charged, semi-surrealist symbolic force, a hovering balance, painstakingly maintained, between the ritual and the real. This, basically, is Ellison's way. This explains, more than anything else, the nature of the reading experience. Single objects and qualities everywhere partake of this charged double vision: the smashed, grinning darky statuette that the hero cannot get rid of; the obscene dancing puppets Clifton is selling at his death; Brother Jack's glass eye in a water tumbler; the ugly black fluid required to maintain the purity of each can of "Optic White"; the lynched figures on Harlem lampposts, who turn out to be bald white shopwindow dummies. There are dozens of such strange symbolic moments.

It is in the extended scenes, however, that Ellison's symbolic artistry is orchestrated to fullest effect. The effect, in the best of these, will be felt even by readers unaware of symbolic design. Such sequences, ideally, maintain a taut, exact, razor's edge balance between ritualism and realism. When one scale of the double standard is up and the other down, when one begins to overweigh the other, something less than perfect results. The Golden Day episode, a sort of *Peer Gynt* madhouse fantasia in which a mob of demented war veterans over-

116

comes its keeper Supercargo (= Superego?) and beats him to unconsciousness, is too patently symbolic, even allegorical, too arranged and theoretical—for all its hysterical energy. The Brotherhood episodes, on the other hand, are perhaps too flatly real. Some readers may find the paint factory sequence and the Rinehart transformations overweighted towards symbolic significance. But with such things as the battle royal, the dispossession, the hero's attempt to lose the Nigger-dummy, I think no one would quarrel. In each he maintains an uncannily packed duplicity, fully real and fully ritual. Each tells the story of America's dilemma in a single crystalline scene. The proof lies in the double fact that each scene seems hypnotically, ineluctably right; but that one is never, while reading, led to suspect the author of symbolist intent.

Best of all may be the chapter called "Out of the Hospital and Under the Bar," which was omitted from the published novel.* Here the hero, after his disastrous explosion at Liberty Paints, is imprisoned in an antiseptic glass case and operated on by voices and white hands which rearrange his brain and identity with electric devices. A Negro maid, a wonderful woman, helps him to escape, into underground passages as psychological as they are architectural. He comes up, finally, through the cellar of a bar, naked into the streets of Harlem, ready for the next stage of his adventures.

The total effect of this sequence cannot be described: it is the story of Negro life in America. It is a genuine nightmare as necessary as those of Samuel Beckett's

---

* It is printed for the first time in the Herbert Hill anthology, *Soon, One Morning.*

trilogy, and as symbolically profound; it is as solid as a Harlem street. It is purely dream and purely real. The perfect meeting is achieved, in art as deft, as balanced, as exhaustive as anything in the book. It is Ellison at his best.

If his best is as good as this, why is he only the finest American *Negro* novelist? He has only written the one novel, for one thing—and that fourteen years ago. Most critics ask more evidence before voting. Secondly, over-consciousness of his effects, while it may not detract from their vivacity, does limit the fullness of their power. Kafka always seemed not to know what he was doing. Somewhere in all the high tension leading up to the riots a center of calm was needed, moreover, and was never provided. Fourthly, and most damaging to Ellison's "place," I suspect, is the disastrously dull imbalance of the second half—250 pages of gray, quasi-communist conspiracies, during which the high fantasy dissolves, the charged edginess is blunted. All this dates, it dries, it cracks.

Ellison's own verdict on his future place is interesting; its modesty, you will note, is importantly qualified.

"I noticed, incidentally, that the Germans, having no special caste assumptions concerning American Negroes, dealt with my work simply as a novel. I think the Americans will come to view it that way in twenty years—if it's around that long."

"Don't you think it will be?"

"I doubt it. It's not an important novel. I failed of eloquence, and many of the immediate issues are rapidly fading away. If it does last, it will be simply because there are things going on in its depth

118

that are of more permanent interest than on its surface." *

To say the least. His proper tradition *is* that of the
great American novelists, as he so hoped it would be,
and it is among them, rather than among the New Negroes, that he should be judged. Hawthorne and Mel-
ville, certainly, are of the family, and Faulkner and
Fitzgerald: all the great ironists of the double vision,
the half-romantic, half-cynical creators and retailers of
the corrupted American dream. They are all symbolic
artists, who charged their objects and events and effects
with preternatural significance, who designed their fictions into national myths. He is not up *there*, of course;
but I see no reason not to assign him a place—even for
one unbalanced book—at least in the high second rank,
with such other ironic idealists as Sherwood Anderson
or Nathanael West. *

BALDWIN

Each of James Baldwin's three novels has been written out of some personal necessity of the author's, a necessity which it describes, conveys, and, hopefully, en-
ables the author to transcend. Everything he writes—
when he writes well—bears this sense of an inner necessity, of the whole of himself told and overcome. From no
other contemporary author does one get such a sensation
of writing as life; it is all so open and desperate and

---

* From *Writers at Work, The Paris Review Interviews*, Second Series
(New York, 1963); also in Ellison's *Shadow and Act*.
* In a poll of two hundred authors, critics, and editors late in 1965,
Invisible Man was voted the American novel "the most memorable and
likely to endure" of the past twenty years.

119

acute, minute by minute and word by word. The captivation of the reader, the feeling of rightness comes from Baldwin's absolute honesty, from his yielding, however unwillingly, to necessity. A reader *feels* the desperation —if the man had not written this book, and written it so, he could not have survived. Each book is a renewed effort to stay alive and upright through the finding and placing of perfect words. Each book is a staving off of death, a matter of survival.

If this is the case, it can scarcely be considered illegitimate or extra-literary prying to regard the novels as essentially about him, the man, James Baldwin. Autobiographical exactness, after all, is the very source of their sting, their astringent modern taste. It is not anti-literary, therefore, or anti-poetic, to talk of *James Baldwin's* family, or experience, or pain, in these novels, rather than John's or David's. It is no more nasty to write of his inversion than of Proust's. When a writer makes it so clear that he is not lying, one should do him the honor of believing him.

There is more than one kind of honesty in writing, of course. A self-dissolving symbolist may tell truth as well as a self-displaying realist, and Baldwin's honesty is only his, the latest variety: the need to tell "all" the truth, with no pretenses, no fictions, no metaphors—the quality one associates with his best essays. Such a need (cf. Mailer, Genet) may ultimately render unusable all the standard props of fiction. In this new, needful, stripped-bare kind of nervous truth, one tells far more than is customarily told, in order to stay this side of insanity. Baldwin allows himself, for example, none of Ellison's objectivity, very little of his distance from his fictions. Like Richard Wright, ultimately, he is probably more a symbolic Negro than a typical one; but, again, like Richard Wright, he is no less useful, or even less necessary, for that.

Each novel, for Baldwin, has been a stage; a stage to be lived through, transformed into words, then exorcised and transcended. The next novel begins a new stage, and the process goes on. This does not, of course, mean that he will ever reach the shores of fulfillment and rest. It seems, in fact, highly unlikely, unless he should begin to lie.

Go Tell It on the Mountain (1952) was the first stage, Baldwin's baptism of fire. It is the testament of his coming to terms with, his defining and transcending, the experience of his boyhood—his family, his religion, his Harlem youth. (The story is told again in "Notes of a Native Son"; it is told a third time, far less honestly, in *The Fire Next Time*.) The telling was necessary for Baldwin, in the same way that telling *Look Homeward, Angel* was necessary for Thomas Wolfe. *Go Tell It on the Mountain* has, in fact, much the same kind of effect as Wolfe's great novel, the effect of autobiography-as-exorcism, of a lyrical, painful, ritual exercise whose necessity and intensity the reader feels. The impact on a reader, in books of this sort, appears to be in direct relation to the amount of truth the author is able to tell himself. At the end of *Go Tell It on the Mountain*, the hero, John, has "come through"; one presumes that Baldwin had as well.

The frame story plays out inside the soul of a fifteen-year-old Negro boy. He is the perfect adolescent author-in-embryo: striving and sensitive, feverish with dreams, pitifully trying to figure it all out. The narrative tells,

121

in rhapsodic Scriptural language, of his desperate fight for faith and salvation against a background of family life in the Harlem ghetto. The family about him— father, mother, brother, and sister—is shredded by violent love-hate combats, pressed by "the weight of white people in the world," as Baldwin calls it, and then driven by their own thwarted senses of right and wrong. They beat because they can't afford to love, they beat their own kind because they have no way of getting at the enemy. When they *do* love they cannot admit it. Their lives are, of necessity, lies, and all release must come from sex, from religious ardor, or from blunt, simple violence—which three, as the novel proves, may all be much the same thing.

John's dreams and visions are shaped by the Lamb's-Blood and Hell Fire faith of his father's militant "Temple of the Fire Baptized," a Negro fortress against the White Outside. Inside the fort, one can pray and chant away the unbearable this-worldly truths in the avenging tones of Scripture: "How long, O Lord holy and true, dost thou not judge and avenge our blood on them that dwell on the earth?" In the final chapter, "The Threshing Floor," John wrestles with innumerable angels in the ordeal of his conversion, a possessive fantasy created by Baldwin from the images of Hell and the Holy Ghost, and emerges wasted, triumphant, and washed in the Blood of the Lamb.

Set into this frame story by the handsome structural device of the second chapter are the intersecting histories of his aunt, his father, and his mother, which give to John's story a deep dimension of history and humanity. The reminiscences of each relative grow out of and blend into their prayers at an evening service,

122

till the reader can finally fit all the pieces of the family
story together. These past histories have the lyric, pri-
mordial, good-and-evil, sex-and-God quality of one of
those hundred-times-told Faulknerian family sagas.
One forgets the details, the genealogy of suffering and
sin and bastardy, and remembers only the tone—a dry,
hollow nostalgia.

It is remarkable how forcibly the background is kept
background in this little book, however pressing its possibilities for development. It is purposely kept a "small"
book—young John's short story (and, to explain it, his
family's)—even an unfinished one, carefully, unforc-
edly told. To hear it one must see, as John sees, all the
reality of ghetto life: the fumey jelly roll of black folks'
sinning, the ambiguous fury of their holiness; one must
hear, as he hears, of lynchings and rapes and beatings.
But all this is unaggressive; it remains a carefully held-
down background that never juts into jarring high re-
lief. All the race truths and war truths are no less "real"
for this containment; they may in fact be more convincing, for the honest casualness of presentation, working
on the reader like subliminal persuasion. Baldwin had
a small, tight, private story to relate, and refused to be
distracted by explosions in the background.

The effect is true, and therefore small—truncated,
incomplete. The loving, voluptuous style, a rhetoric of
rocking prose rhythms stolen from Negro song and
Negro sermon (half or more of the book is chanted in
Scriptural cadences, graven in Scriptural imagery) may
not vary enough to sustain a two hundred-page narrative. (Then again, such "tediousness" may only occur
to unwilling, non-participating readers.) Baldwin is as
unafraid of glorious prose as he is of honest prose, and

123

the book is woven out of both. But the strength, at last, is that of his own personal necessity, a necessity that the reader can vicariously share. It is the strength of a harrowing prayer, simple and felt, of a small tragic truth that enlarges the heart. The book is carven with love. Because of its peculiar kind of necessary, very personal truth, it remains one of the few, the very few, essential Negro works.

Giovanni's Room (1956) served its purpose too, I suspect. Baldwin's personal uncertainties are not limited to the racial, religious, and familial. It is the story of a latent American homosexual (white, very confused) discovering the truth about himself in Paris at the hands of an attractive Italian barman; the barman, Giovanni, stands as a sort of symbolic, anti-Anglo Saxon pagan. The American attempts to elude the painful discovery in the arms of his fiancée, but he soon gives up the struggle, lapses into sailors, and is left drifting towards the life of an aging queer.

It is certainly one of the most subtle novels of the homosexual world, not as poetic and outspoken as Genet's, not as trashy as John Rechy's; but the emotions are more to be observed than to be shared. It has something of the lyrical allusiveness of *Go Tell It on the Mountain*, of its squeezing, sonnetlike smallness—Giovanni's room is the perfect symbolic setting, as cluttered and oppressively closed as one of Pinter's settings. But the effect, on the whole, is slight. The hero may protest too much. By contrast with the novels on either side, the "truth" seems too fictionalized. Something has been averted, held at arm's length. The issue of Baldwin's homosexuality was to be thrashed out again in *Another Country*, and we may not have heard the end of it yet.

In this latest novel (1963), Baldwin becomes more stridently clear: a hyperexcited, overshrill, wide-open New York City voice has replaced the old Paris one, and the result is a key document in the race war, a crucial American novel.

Another Country, and the sick truths it tells Americans about themselves, had to wait for the emergence of a new style: a style one may designate as New York-1960's, on the presumptions that it will, by sheer fury, have worn itself out by the seventies, and that it becomes alien and dilute off Manhattan Island, where it was born. It is used, at its shrillest, most wide-open, by Baldwin, Edward Albee, LeRoi Jones, Norman Mailer, Lenny Bruce, *The Realist*, the new Grove Press novelists, some of the Jewish Establishment journalists and critics (*The New York Review*, *The New Leader*, *Partisan Review*), and probably by hundreds of New Yorkers whose names we will never know. It has correspondences with softer manifestations like pop art, Jules Feiffer, Nichols and May, *A Hard Day's Night*. Jane, Vivaldo's "beat chick" in *Another Country*, is a splendid specimen: she is brittle, bitchy, fresh from the shrink, with sex like broken glass; a frenzied neurotic with every nerve bare and bleeding loud, first cousin to Lula in *The Dutchman*.

This style almost entirely carries the book, a style of screaming, no-holds-barred verbal violence. The revolving sequence of events, the inter-ringing figures of the sex dance (everyone mixing with everyone else), even, ultimately, the characters in the dance themselves, white and black, homo-, hetero-, and bi-sexual, exist primarily to provide voices and vehicles for the screamy exchanges, the ear-piercing insults, the excru-

ciating displays of mutual torment. Scenes are carved
in blue fire, each character lashing out viciously at the
others. Not only is love impossible in this new world
(except between perfectly matched homosexuals), so
too, apparently, is the avoidance of this white-hot, sado-
masochistic fury. It is as if the author had no other
means of revealing his characters' psychology.

Not surprisingly, most of this violence is racial. By
setting a novel full of cool, case-hardened New Yorkers—primarily underground New Yorkers, writers,
drifters, jazzmen, and the like—Baldwin has provided
himself with a cast of characters as likely to speak their
honest minds as unrepressed three-year-olds. Two
black-and-white liaisons (Rufus and Leona, then Rufus' sister Ida and Vivaldo—the second simply repeats
the first, *da capo, molto vivace*) provide him with scores
of occasions for the most vitriolic displays of color-
mania, in which the Negroes inevitably have the last
and loudest word. I had thought Rufus Scott so slash-
ingly violent, so incredibly, masochistically sensitive
about his skin color that his equal for venom was not
to be found. Then, after his suicide, I met his sister:
pure spitfire, her veins all electric, born with a snake
whip in her mouth for the lashing of whites.

The race war, as depicted in this novel, is a difficult
thing to understand. First of all, Baldwin has almost
entirely excluded "average" people, the simple white
American bourgeoisie or lower orders, whose prejudice
is so obvious and so stupid it bores even more than it
disgusts him. The few representatives of *that* world,
the upstairs world, who foolishly drop into the plot are
usually dissolved into steam with single drops of acid.
(A pair of white heterosexual liberals, the Silenskis,

so square they are married and have children and make money, degenerate into the crudest samples of sick America before the book is through, despite Baldwin's obvious efforts to be fair. Their racial liberality, it develops, is as fragile as their sexual assurance. So much for "normal" people.)

So all we have left to fight the race war are a few outlaw blacks and highly emancipated whites. In such a context the war loses its social relevance (except perhaps symbolically), and takes on the dimensions of a private duel. But the issues are no less clear. "Somewhere in his heart the black boy hated the white boy because he was white. Somewhere in his heart Vivaldo had hated and feared Rufus because he was black." Baldwin tries, or at least the top of his mind tries, to keep the sides equal, and the fighting fair. The white combatants, Leona, Vivaldo, especially Eric, are created with affection and care: these are no evil, ill-understood Wrighteous puppets. But the Negroes have all the trumps. It is *they*, always, who carry the whip, and no white lover, friend, or reader dares to deny them the right. Ida, for example, sees an insult in every white look, and our invisible narrator (James Baldwin) insists that she is right:

> . . . she was always waiting for the veiled insult or the lewd suggestion. And she had good reason for it, she was not being fantastical or perverse. It was the way the world treated girls with bad reputations, and every colored girl had been born with one.

This is not Ida talking. However "liberal" he may think himself, any white person in this setting is pa-

127

thetic. The best one can afford him is a redress of sympathy for being so hopelessly at the mercy of his black master or mistress. Either the sides *are* in fact morally stacked in favor of the Negro in America, or Baldwin has so stacked them in this novel.

At their most intense, these race-war combats always transmute into sex combats—which illustrates Baldwin's theory of the fundamentally sexual character of racism. This aspect of the novel, however, is even more unsettled and unsettling, because of the case Baldwin is trying to make for inversion.

The usual American formulation of the race war in sexual terms is that all Negroes are fantastically potent wizards of sex with prodigious genitals, appetites, and abilities; all whites are confused, impotent little sexual rejects, proper citizens of the world's most sexually confused, most sexually obsessed, puritan/prurient country. It is to compensate for this presumed imbalance, in Baldwin's theory, that the whole system of segregation, race hate, and dehumanization was established by the master race, comforted by its ten-to-one superiority in numbers. The Negro, conversely, has to rest content with the sexual superiority the whites insist he possesses.

Not only does Baldwin allow his characters to adopt this formulation—Ida is a past master at the white-emasculating insult—he seems to accept it implicitly himself. (See the quotation on page 5 of this essay.) He implants the notion (e.g., Vivaldo's "subtle failure" with Ida) that there *is* a significant difference between the white man's performance and the Negro's. On one occasion—it must be the root symbolic gesture of the race war—Vivaldo and a Negro friend compare penises. For all his genuine affection for his white hero, this is one contest Baldwin cannot afford to let Vivaldo win.

His allegiance to the compensatory myth of the macrogenitals is not, of course, Baldwin's only realm of sexual confusion, or his novel's. His general picture of sex in America (as represented by marginal "normal" people: the Silenskis, Greenwich Village lovers) is fairly ghastly, all dry and mechanical and guilty. Copulation is described in terms of riding, thrusting, beating. The so-called act of love is portrayed with all the delight of an abortion in reverse.

This applies, however, only to heterosexual affairs. Behind all this grunting cacaphony there sings, through the book, the pure violin note of a homosexual idyll. The silvery sea episode of Eric and Yves on the Mediterranean that opens Book II; the Genet-like rhapsody of love between Eric and Vivaldo that opens Book III, described in full poetic detail; Eric's memory of Rufus: *this* is love, this is blue-eyed perfection. The language softens to tender whispers of incredible sweetness, and one wonders if the odds have not been unfairly disturbed. The one time the white race gains, momentarily, the upper hand, is when Ida starts condescending to queers; she sounds just like a white liberal pitying the poor coloreds, and the roles are reversed: a white homosexual, in Baldwin's formula, has the same moral superiority over the enemy that a Negro has. As for a *Negro* homosexual . . . ! The over-lyrical poeticizing of homosexual love is one of the real flaws of the book. Surely Genet's pictures, or even Baldwin's in *Giovanni's*

Room, of the foul *and* fair of inversion, are more just. This is, obviously, a new Baldwin. There will be others. *Another Country* has, in its frantic new writer's world called New York, much of the same necessity, the same quality of desperate exorcism as Baldwin's earlier works. But things here are less under control. Almost all of the thinking, the non-imaginative thinking of Baldwin's essays is sandwiched into the fiction, bearing a suggestion that the man is now writing more from his ideas than his imagination. The piercing one-note tone of repetitiousness of so much of this long book supports this dissatisfying notion. Another dangerous sign is the confusion of narrative authority, very like the confusions of self-identity which mar so many of Baldwin's latest and weakest essays. His own opinions mingle with those of his characters, subjectivity jars with objectivity in such a way as to indicate that the author is unaware of the difference: i.e., that James Baldwin, through the 1950's the sole master of *control* in American prose, in the 1960's has begun to lose control.

What is there to salvage and prize? A number of things. More often than not, between the explosions, *Another Country* reminds the reader that James Baldwin is still one of the genuine stylists of the English language. Consider the opening nocturne, of Rufus walking the streets of New York; or Ida's debut as a jazz singer; or the frantic literary cocktail party; or Eric's *Si le grain ne meurt* reminiscence of an Alabama boyhood; or the stunning set piece of the Museum of Modern Art, a perfect specimen of the monstrously real New York that is the secret hero of more than one great modern novel:

They reached the first of a labyrinthine series of rooms, shifting and crackling with groups of people, with bright paintings above and around them, and stretching into the far distance, like tombstones with unreadable inscriptions. The people moved in waves, like tourists in a foreign graveyard. Occasionally, a single mourner, dreaming of some vanished relationship, stood alone in adoration or revery before a massive memorial—but they mainly evinced, moving restlessly here and there, the democratic gaiety. Cass and Eric moved in some panic through this crowd, trying to find a quieter place; through fields of French impressionists and cubists and cacophonous modern masters, into a smaller room dominated by an enormous painting, executed, principally, in red, before which two students, a girl and a boy, stood holding hands. . . .

They passed not far from a weary guard, who looked blinded and dazzled, as though he had never been able to escape the light. Before them was a large and violent canvas in greens and reds and blacks, in blocks and circles, in daggerlike exclamations; it took a flying leap, as it were, from the wall, poised for the spectator's eyeballs; and at the same time it seemed to stretch endlessly and adoringly in on itself, reaching back into an unspeakable chaos. It was aggressively and superbly uncharming and unreadable, and might have been painted by a lonely and bloodthirsty tyrant, who had been cheated of his victims. "How horrible," Cass murmured, but she did not move; for they had this corner, except for the guard, to themselves.

There are moments, too—especially towards the end of the novel—when Baldwin shows himself a worthy heir of Proust, suavely analyzing the mixed motives of lovers in pairs and threes and fours, their whirlpools of self-torment over the feelings of others. Eric, in particular, is so poignantly honest it wounds. And the conclusions of the book, Ida's conclusion, Eric's conclusion, are not only genuine but, for once, sympathetic and humane.

Still, all these make up—what? five percent? ten percent? of the book. Most of what we have to fall back on, finally, is the same bed of nails we began with, that four hundred-page torture in a new-New York accent. And what good, even to a white man, is a bed of nails?

As of all "painful" works, no one reader can speculate how useful the pain may be for another. One may ask whether it is "realistic"—where there *are* such people? Baldwin, in this novel, has convinced me there are, and that they are not always the freakishly odd exceptions. The book strikes me, moreover, as precisely and exactly of its time and of its place, as much so as other honest, unfictionlike American novels such as *Herzog* or Clancy Sigal's *Going Away*. What its real value for Americans will prove, I think, for Americans who can separate the good from the bad—like so many Negro works, it is a remarkably "American" book—is that of the first open and direct statement, however unpleasant, of some underlying psychological truths of the race war, and of much else that is wrong with America as well. It reads like a record of the climactic sessions in a long, national psychoanalysis—*here* is what is really wrong, it seems to cry, for all of its own confusion, a many-men's sickness that only *one* man has been able to define, out loud.

Such a statement, as I say, had to await the national near crack-up of the sixties before it could find voice. As people are likely to retreat rather quickly from such dangerously deep honesty—Baldwin seems lately to be retreating himself—it would perhaps be well for Americans to try to listen now to the noise of *Another Country*, and of Baldwin generally; and to judge for themselves just how much of a share they have in the judgment. *Is* it only his disease being uncovered? Or something more?

The stories of *Going to Meet the Man* (1965) were evidently written at different stages in Baldwin's career, and many of their effects depend on interreflections back and forth with the earlier works. Some stories borrow the voice and setting of *Go Tell It on the Mountain;* others the jagged, brittle tones, the Manhattan underground world of *Another Country*. Many echo the essays, too, and there are even tastes of the whining, bullying rant of *The Fire Next Time*, the flip self-importance of the Mailer essay, the turgid speculations of *Nothing Personal*.

Of the weak, or perverse, or merely dispensable stories—four out of eight, which is certainly respectable —two are appendices to *Go Tell It on the Mountain*, with the same hero and his family, roughly the same manner and tone, although with almost nothing of the novel's harrowing, cathartic effect. Least impressive are "Previous Condition" and "This Morning, This Evening, So Soon," both of which represent the worst of

the several James Baldwins: the pretentious, near-para-
noiac, picked-on Negro, ostentatiously bearing all the
sufferings of his race. In both cases, a clue is the total
lack of detachment between the author and his chip-on-
the-shoulder narrative heroes. The suffering, self-pity-
ing voice is a sign of James Baldwin's least controlled
and least valuable fiction.

Of the four better pieces, "Sonny's Blues" hovers
delicately in tone between *Go Tell It on the Mountain*
and *Another Country*. It is a small, artless, ambling
story, one weak man's memory of his brother: the
account of his long attempt to understand his brother
Sonny, a junkie turned jazz pianist in Harlem, so
quietly and uncertainly told that it is almost not a story
at all, but just the telling, the trying: a confession that
drifts coolly and unhurriedly through digression and
reminiscence.

"Come Out of the Wilderness," at the opposite extreme, is a dazzling display of Baldwin's style at its
sharpest. Its prose surface has a bristly, electric exactness, its dialogue the bright newness of good talk. The
story, an open and unprejudiced playing through of the
odi et amo tensions of an affair, seems a distillate of all
that is best in *Another Country*. It has the same crackling Manhattan setting, the same crouching-cat tension.
It has something new and surprising to say about the
races. And it offers a cool, cruel analysis of the self-
deluding stratagems of lovers, a microscopic plotting
of our bitchy little hearts.

"The Man Child" is something entirely new for
Baldwin, a highly charged, lyrical, pastoral tragedy.
Four people—a boy, his father, his father's friend, his

mother—are frozen in a mythic isolation. Their story grows, the trap tightens, slowly and expansively, through incremental repetitions, incantatory rhythms, the loving simple cadences of a legend.

The title story, "Going to Meet the Man," is Baldwin's second attempt to imagine sympathetically the mind of a Southern white bigot. I found his picture to be credible, intense, and at times almost hypnotically convincing: everything that *Blues for Mister Charlie* was not. It is basically a lynching story, of which there are literally dozens of examples in Negro literature. But this is the first to be drawn from the point of view of a more or less sympathetic observer, the Southern deputy sheriff as a young boy. As the boy's anticipation turns to a strange kind of horrified fulfillment, the reader may find himself forced to admit that there *is* in this barbaric, anti-human rite a genuine primeval satisfaction—a disturbing, very Baldwinesque lesson.

This is not the place for a full discussion of Baldwin's non-fictional work. It is a subject I would one day like to consider with care, but until I have extracted myself more from the highly personal implications of his themes, I will confine myself to the safety of a few notes on his style.

He is the most powerful and important American essayist of the postwar period, perhaps of the century. *Notes of a Native Son* and *Nobody Knows My Name* will maintain their place among the small collection of genuine American classics. They have already been adopted as standard texts and models of style in American college courses; and this is not just a "vogue," an offshoot of the Civil Rights movement. Two such books would sustain any reputation, as long as men can tell the true from the false.

Baldwin begins, in these essays, with a simple desire, a desire turned commitment: "I want to be an honest man and a good writer." He concludes with the keenest analysis of the American dilemma since Alexis de Tocqueville. It is the most difficult job in the world to avoid lying, lying in any form, while writing on urgent matters: to avoid false rhetoric, stylish language, to avoid the self-deluding fine phrases with which a writer can so easily plaster over the cracks in a sentence or a thought. Baldwin has shown more concern for the painful exactness of prose style than any other modern American writer. He picks up words with heavy care, then sets them, one by one, with a cool and loving precision that one can feel in the reading. There are no bright words in his best essays, no flashes, allusions, delusions, no Tynanesque "brilliance." His style is like stripped conversation, saying the most that words can *honestly* say. If it hurts, if it ties one down and hammers its words on one's mind, it is simply the effect of his won't-let-go rigor. There is good and bad prose, there is moral and immoral.

This does not of course imply that the style is flat, because it is not like champagne. Baldwin is fully aware of the ambiguities and ironies implicit in his subjects (primary among them the sick paradox that calls itself America), and he weaves these same ambiguities and ironies into his prose. He is also drivingly and constantly self-critical, which is why his writing is so strong and clear, his thinking so often unassailable. His paragraphs work like a witty colloquy of two sharp minds, Baldwin's and his critic's, one within the other: the devastating qualifiers, the cool understatements, the parentheses, the litotes, the suggestions and quiet parallels display the double mind of the self-critic at work.

Writing like this can be more harrowing, more intense than *any* of the works we are considering. As Baldwin himselfs admits, Negro literature "is more likely to be a symptom of our tension than an examination of it," and this includes his own three novels, his plays, and his stories. The exhilarating exhaustion of reading his best essays—which in itself may be a proof of their honesty and value—demands that the reader measure up, and forces him to learn.

VII

NEGRO WRITERS TODAY:
THE NOVELISTS II

Leaving these three, one moves into a distinctly different air, one considerably easier to breathe. It does no injustice to the several other meritorious Negro novelists working to confess that none of them approaches Wright, Ellison, or Baldwin in significance. So far, public opinion has been just. I shall call attention to a small number of them, and make a special plea for Ann Petry. But we are visiting in a different region now, and it will do no one service to overstate its claims.

In considering their novels, the problem of better and worse becomes formidable. Anyone, it is assumed, can write a novel, anyone with a way with words and a story to tell. For Negroes, nowadays, whose stories are exciting and controversial and vendible, even the way with words may be disposed of. This assumption has resulted in a number of "Supposed Confessions of a Second-Rate Sensitive Mind," to borrow a title of Tennyson's, which creates two problems for the reader-interpreter-critic. First, there is the problem of reading. The ability to read bad books easily is restricted to the uncritically absorbent escapist or the patient scholar, to very small minds or very great ones. Secondly, there is the problem of assessment. There are obstacles enough, as we have seen, to an American white reader's assessing *any* sample of Negro writing, due to the intervening fogs of race guilt and moral intimidation. Read the doctrinaire, white-liberal reviews of Negro protest novels: the worst of such novels elicit stock responses of dutiful, misdirected praise.

But there are obstacles as well, guilt or no guilt, to evaluating even the informational content. How honest or representative, or even symbolically true, can one assume the writing of small-minded men to be? The vision of Negro life afforded by short-sighted, unimaginative Negro novelists may well be more distorted than that of the intelligent white reader himself. Mere blackness is no certificate of expertness, on "Negro life" or on anything else, no Key to the Mystery. White critics and readers, so anxious for the key, too often accept each Negro in print as a teacher, even when the lessons contradict. Negro writers protest, legitimately, the many suave white race experts who presume to instruct them as to the nature of Negroes. But a white man, too, should be on his guard against Negroes who presume too assertively to speak for The Race. Too few speak for more than themselves, and if the self is undistinguished or mean, there is no reason on earth to take it for either specimen or guide.

> . . . for a writer to insist that his personal suffering is of special interest in itself, or simply because he belongs to a particular racial or religious group, is to advance a claim for special privileges which members of his group who are not writers would be ashamed to demand.
>
> (Ralph Ellison)

How then are such novels to be used? The distinction between dynamic, activist writing, first, and the "pure," self-sufficient work should probably be allowed to remain. The former may be granted its chance to wound

139

and arouse, in the scales of each reader's conscience. Such books—"protest novel" is really an inadequate term—usually offer either a supposedly typical case study (*The Street*) or a broad survey (*Youngblood*) of Negro suffering under white oppression, in semi-documentary fashion; or a more symbolic, secondary rendering of this suffering and oppression through a display of the anger and hatred they produce, either in the style itself, in the story told, or in a character (*If He Hollers Let Him Go*). In either case, the tale is designed not to teach rationally, but to excite, passionately. It is the conscientious white reader's job to measure himself against the indictment implied, to decide whether or not the pain induced is legitimate, and to use it if it is.

Ultimately, the distinctions between active and pure, between more and less useful, like the distinction between better and worse, depend on the reader's own moral and intellectual capacities—Negro writing so often seems a test of the reader more than of the country as a whole. Small souls will be intimidated by the most unbalanced indictments, just as small minds will accept the most distorted "information," and small imaginations be enraptured by the most artless fictions.

The more sophisticated a white reader, morally and imaginatively, the more magnanimous and wise, the more resistant will he be to the lower orders of Negro writing, whether that writing be designed to wound, to instruct, or to entertain.

Poor writing will reach its proper audience, and attain its proper effect: its flabby readers will writhe, be misinformed, and be titillated—all briefly, and ineffectually. From the weakly written Negro novel, a careful reader will realize that he is often learning not about

Negroes, but about weak Negro writers. He ought not, thereby, to ignore such novels entirely. On the assumption that there is something to be learned from every man's story, he may glean what is genuine—details of setting, evidence of popular fancies and fixations, the data of one small man's dreams and experiences—and discard what is spurious or pretentious. Small men suffer too, he will learn, and he may, he just may have been in some way responsible for that suffering.

But he will realize that it is only the objective, the generous, the capacious of soul who can know other men truly—even other Negroes, who after all are as ornery and irreducible as any other men; and that it is only the patient and painstaking artist who can communicate this knowledge. Any pain such writers induce is likely to be legitimate and warranted. Unfortunately, America has granted few of her Negro writers the physical or psychological leisure for such luxuries as generosity, objectivity, magnanimity, and art; and has reaped a harvest of subjective, small-souled, belligerent, and artless Negro novels. Of these—and the discrimination of course does not apply to all—I shall mention only some of the better, better known, or useful.

A first group, the most celebrated of the second rank, might be regarded as the School of Wright—although the tradition of Negro protest fiction predates him by many years, and for some of these authors no direct connection to Wright could be traced. These are the specifically "angry" novels, the sort Irving Howe thought all Negroes should be writing; they are symptoms of the race war, to adopt Baldwin's distinction, rather than examinations. They are weapons; like rock-filled mudballs, they are aimed from the Negro fort into the white fort, in the hope of wounding or at least splattering some of its inhabitants.

Chester Himes was a close associate of Richard Wright's in Paris. Although he is now, according to the publicity, at work on his fifteenth book—a number of these have been popular thrillers—it is still the first, *If He Hollers Let Him Go* (1945), that warrants attention. It is set in a southern California shipyard in wartime (war projects, because of the need for workers, were one of the first large-scale instances in America of unsegregated hiring); the hero is race-mad almost to the point of hysteria, packed with dry high explosive, waiting for the match. He eases the almost unbearable tension of being Negro by speeding a powerful car down the freeways or by insulting his lighter-colored, educated, upper-middle-class fiancée and her friends. (Himes' treatment of classes and groups he does not like, like that of many angry writers, proves them to be also classes and groups he does not know.) He very nearly kills a white co-worker over an insult, then becomes embroiled in a sex duel with a trashy white female, who both despises and desires him. The climax occurs when she locks him in a room with her and screams rape—a ritual scene in Negro novels. Beaten and defeated, he escapes with his life.

Himes' subsequent novels play cruder variations on the race-war theme. In *Lonely Crusade* (1947) he mixed in heavy doses of a communism that made the novel more attractive to European than American tastes. *The Third Generation* (1954) is the sordid, late-naturalist chronicle of the utter decay of an entire Negro family, under the pressure of a light-colored, cannibalistic mother who despises her black husband and his race. The book's harrowing frenzy suggests that Himes may have been settling some long-rankling childhood scores. Most recently, in *Pinktoes* (1965), Himes has turned to the newly profitable genre of Olympia/Grove Press comic pornography, asserting his status as a highly commercial writer. The book is an interracial sex fantasy that reviewers will call "wildly funny." It is the kind of thing, in Dr. Johnson's phrase, that anyone could go on writing indefinitely, "if he would but abandon his mind to it."

James Oliver Killens has written two long, detailed, humorless, artless, almost documentary race novels, *Youngblood* (1954) and *And Then We Heard the Thunder* (1963). The first is a sort of Negro family epic, the expected tale of two generations of long-suffering blacks and their sadistic white masters in a Georgia town. The second tells the interminable story of Negroes (and whites) in wartime, where the ordeal of World War II seems less harrowing, in the long run, than the race war inside it. It runs through pages of somber "graphic realism," i.e., pages of vapidly obscene barracks chatter and hard-boiled crudeness of description: that's the way it was. Both books are sincerely well intended, and packed to bursting with details of Negro (Southern, army) life, episode after episode, as retailed by a careful, intelligent, unimaginative Negro with absolutely no sense of the art of fiction. They represent the kind of novel most Americans with great stocks of experience would probably write, if they had the will and were Negroes. The books are useful, and, to readers who make no great demands on their novelists, mildly moving and exciting.

Carl Offord's *The White Face* (1943) is a Harlem-set story involving heroic white communists, Negro anti-Semitism, a fake accusation of rape, mass rallies, and the brutalizing underworld of police and criminal corruption. It is less flat than Killens' epics, with more jagged ups and downs; if incredible, it is still readable. The pathetic family of Southern *émigré* Negroes at the center, used, degraded, finally ruined by both left and right, lingers in the imagination and gnaws, for all the contrivance of their plot, at the reader's social conscience.

Several other Negroes have written in this most obvious, least artful, least demanding fashion, mostly in the forties, with less success—William G. Smith, Curtis Lucas, George Wylie Henderson, Willard Savoy. The best-selling Willard Motley (*Knock on Any Door*, *We Fished All Night*, *Let No Man Write My Epitaph*) writes voluptuously indulgent farragos of the white underground, violent, artless, sordid, and stupid, each one weaker than the last. Some experience of this collection is useful, of the School of Wright. But most of it is written by small minds, for small minds, regardless of race, color, or creed, and can only scantly repay the intelligent reader.

Langston Hughes is as skillful and durable a storyteller as he is a poet, a master at the ironic little social comedies of Negro life—a type he seems almost to have invented, so sure now is his hold and possession. His work lives as a potent reminder to the critic of the enduring primacy of "the story." He is an ingenious and happy craftsman in the best tradition of Somerset Maugham or O. Henry; his stories can be read, enjoyed, and understood by the man of simple common sense who dwells, presumably, in everyone. It would be folly to condescend; to suggest, effetely, that one is past such things: one never is. There is much to be admired in a small perfect circle. If Langston Hughes' stories are not deeply, endlessly resonant, or are not richly laden with awesome suggestion, they are still honest, deft, amusing, and provocative, reading after reading. They endure. He is lesser than Ellison or Baldwin only because his scope is so much smaller, not because his work is cheaper or less complete. But comparisons are foolish for a writer so attractive and secure.

Hughes has written another novel since *Not Without Laughter*, three collections of stories, and his delightful but utterly unassessable contribution to American (and Negro) folklore, three volumes of the unconventional wisdom and raffish adventures of Jesse B. Simple, the hero of his Chicago *Defender* columns of the fifties. He really "tells stories" rather than writes fiction, and he rarely makes mistakes. Although he has written of many things, his most comfortable subject is the urban Northern American Negro, his jobs, his play, his churches, his women. He can deal with various classes, but seems most at home with the poor. His text for Roy de Carava's rich photo essay, *The Sweet Flypaper of Life* (1955), is as total an example of Langston Hughes, of his bittersweet participation in the lives of his people, as anything else he has written.

145

There seems to be no distance, really, between author and subject, no artist's detachment—which is doubtless the effect of very careful art.

His tone has that intimate, elusive, near-tragic, near-comic sound of the Negro blues, and is equally defiant of analysis. His theme is not so much white oppression, as the Negro's quiet resistance to it. His writings typify (and probably support) the famous and useful myth of Negro endurance—the knowing grin, half-smile half-smirk, of the bowing but unbeaten. They may thus not find favor with more militant Negroes, who regard the very myth of endurance as treacherously pacifist, supported if not invented by whites.

The "Simple" stories, one or two pages long, offer little barbed home truths about Harlem life, the cost of living, domestic unbliss, and especially the various ludicrous paradoxes of America's racial double standard. Jesse B. Simple is a sort of comic no-good (a stereotype turned to use, written by a Negro for Negroes) with perpetual lady troubles, cadging beers off the straight man who tells the stories in exchange for another of his twisty bits of folk wisdom about "the ways of white folks."

On the whole, Hughes' creative life has been as full, as varied, and as original as Picasso's, a joyful, honest monument of a career. There is no noticeable sham in it, no pretension, no self-deceit; but a great, great deal of delight and smiling irresistible wit. If he seems for the moment upstaged by angrier men, by more complex artists, if "different views engage" us, necessarily, at this trying stage of the race war, he may well outlive them all, and still be there when it's over. Much of the greatness of the three major Negro novelists derives from their singularity, their essential aloneness; Hughes' at least seems to derive from his anonymous unity with his people. He *seems* to speak for millions, which is a tricky thing to do.

A few other Negro authors, more obvious, less integrated authors than Langston Hughes, have tried the ironic vein. In the palmy Harlem Renaissance days there were the gross, effective satires of George Schuyler and Wallace Thurman—*Black No More* (1931) and *Infants of the Spring* (1932)—the latter a takeoff on the decadent Renaissance itself. More recently, J. Saunders Redding, in *Stranger and Alone* (1950), depicted with venomous austerity the slow growth and successful career of a typical "Negro Leader." Sheldon Howden, a frightened little orphan student of mixed blood, grows through the Negro college and work circuit to become one of the self-serving, white-run "educators" of his people, as despicable a three-faced sycophant as his protector Wimbush or as Ellison's Dr. Bledsoe. The novel is varied but somewhat flat, academic in more ways than one. Redding's calm control, however, his restraint before the satiric potential is truly admirable; the reader never knows just when it is that the hero shifts allegiance, so subtly is his progress traced from total innocence to total corruption.

The Living is Easy (1948), by Dorothy West, is a raking apart of the Negro middle class of Boston, with its desperate attempts to "rise," to seem white, its holier-than-white disdain for the blacks who are below them. Unfortunately it is wretchedly overwritten, very crudely thought, and quite unconvincing, for all its probable justice. It may prove agreeably shocking to middle-class Negroes, and informative to whites unaware that Negroes have their class distinctions too. But the writer's mind, ultimately, is betrayed as not a great deal more open or more interesting than those of the black bourgeoisie she is satirizing.

There are a number of recent novels of Harlem (or Manhattan) life by Negroes that I have found readable, artful, and memorable. *The Street* (1946) by Ann Petry I shall speak more of shortly: it has a possessive background naturalism that is utterly convincing. Despite its almost unnecessary plot, this book proved Mrs. Petry to be one of the more admirable and skillful of postwar writers. It was read at the time for all the wrong reasons, and classed among the protest novels. In a way it is; it makes a moving case against the New York ghetto. But it is the author's reaching, selfless sympathy that makes the case, a sympathy that allows her to become each character, however vile, each object, in turn; and the effortless, artful irony of her style.

Julian Mayfield's *The Hit* (1957), a small, strangely airy family tragedy, I especially liked. It limits itself to the very average, comically empty stories of a few people—a little Negro building superintendent, his wife, his lady friend, his cab-driver son, the son's girl, a ubiquitous numbers runner—all on a single day; the day of The Hit. The little man, Hubert, has a vision of escape all caught up in Number 417. It hits: four, then one, then seven, for forty-two hundred dollars. He is free, of wife and son and job and all the Harlem gloom, free to fly. He waits and waits. But the numbers man has skipped, his little dream is deferred. What makes the sad story oddly fun is Mayfield's choice economy and craft, as he intersects the little bits of lives with the day's number calls, and his numb, detached way of putting it all down. (The author, after a second novel, emigrated to Africa.)

The Messenger (1963), by Charles Wright, is set more in James Baldwin's New York, that big brittle loveless town of queens and queers and neurotic lonely nights. It is told by a young Negro messenger-boy prostitute who lives in a mixed-up midtown apartment, told by him in cold dry breaths of narrative, with something of Baldwin's own necessary inner honesty, his anti-fictional bent. The episodes are mixed, sweet and sour (mostly sour), discontinuous. The end is just a stopping place. Dimension backwards is afforded by tender memory pieces of a Missouri childhood, of a grandmother's death, of the war in Korea. What we have is a pure, calm, existentially true bit of self-assessment by a very genuine, very sad, very lonely human being. It is a small book—so many good ones seem to be—but the author's sad honesty is touching and rare.

Two of the handsomest "small" novels by American Negroes, modest, self-contained poetic biographies of about two hundred pages, are Owen Dodson's *Boy at the Window* (1951) and Gwendolyn Brooks' *Maud Martha* (1953). Both are genuine, delicate, and sure, written by sensitive artists who are also feeling human beings. Both are wholly appealing to read. In Dodson's book we live a sad-happy year or two with Coin Foreman, a nine-ten-eleven-year-old colored boy from Brooklyn (Dodson's home). During the quick months that we dwell inside his thoughts, many things happen. He gets religion, finds a girl friend, learns he is a "nigger," stares in pain at family quarrels, in bewilderment at adult meanness. His mother sickens and dies. In the lavish emotional confusion of her funeral, the book—

and Coin's mind—swells to its fullest. He sees his father decline, and is packed off to Washington to live with a blind, drinking uncle and his mistress. Here, in the book's closing pages, he encounters sex, fights, makes a friend, and loses him, and his story stops.

It may sound like a hundred other novels of the Sensitive Child Growing Up, but it isn't. The whole thing is done with loving finesse. Dodson weaves private ten-year-old thoughts, remembered and imagined, with adroit adult skill and selectivity, into a narrative that is smoothly unrolling, and all of a piece. It does not condescend, it does not puff up, it is never artificial. The episodic sequences leap softly about, like a dragon-fly on water. The random associations ("Yes We Have No Bananas" keeps twining in Coin's mind with the hymns of his mother's funeral), the inset boy thought and boy talk rarely seem "clever" or contrived.

A story of Dodson's ("Come Home Early, Chile") in Herbert Hill's *Soon, One Morning* picks up Coin, returned from the war, at eighteen. All of ten pages long, the story is (barring perhaps the Ellison fragment) the finest thing in this superior collection. Dodson has not only retained the loving touch of *Boy at the Window*, he now reveals as well an exuberant imagination—his Deaconess Quick may be the largest, most alive, most Dickensian character in all American Negro fiction—and a colloquial, musically witty style that begs to be read aloud. The opening:

> What in the world was Deaconess Quick doing perching on a bar stool. Coin was startled and delighted to see all her great fat way up on high. A pillar of the church, no less, was on that artificial

leather stool tasting, with relish, her beer. Well, bless her soul. As he watched her from his distance, she seemed perfectly at home taking small sips and giggling into her glass. She didn't look to left or right but worked her head to the mirror in front of her with secret smilings and panting joy. Maybe he should go out before she recognized him. As he started toward the door, the familiar voice hit his back like a syphon spraying him. He turned.

"Coin Foreman, well now you know. You mean you weren't going to say the word to me . . . I'm ashamed, honey. Yes, I'm ashamed, you know, that you wouldn't press my heart after all these years. Come here, honey, now you know, and say a word." Coin stood at attention. "I ain't ashamed, honey, I learned long ago about the eat, drink and be merry, which is in the *Bible*, Lord."

The people in the room looked first at Coin and then at her and held their laughter in. She was ridiculous as an Easter hat fashioned of paper roses and colored eggs. That's what she had on too. And a violet dress flowered with poppies. She looked like a field held on high. And laughed with fat joy. Her bosoms bloomed toward the bar and settled in satisfaction when Coin walked to her. Getting down from the stool she was a parade of flirtation and arthritis. Now she held him in her arms kissing beer into his cheeks and onto his newly pressed uniform. "Home again, home again," she said. He breathed into her old softness. She patted him into childhood and sobbed the past into his chest. "Here he come, a grown man into my arms. Now you know, that's nice. A old lady is blessed to see you, to see thee. Coin, he has returned to me."

Maud Martha is a striking human experiment, as exquisitely written and as effective as any of Gwendolyn Brooks' poetry in verse. In thirty-four tiny fragments, vignettes, tiny moments in passage, the reader skims into the life of Maud Martha. First we meet a seven-year-old fat brown girl nobody loves enough; then a dreaming adolescent suffering through dates, living in her books and her satiny visions (the wrong hair, the wrong color, even for a Negro); then the young bride, in a minute kitchenette in a sad gray building in a cold white world, joined to her small-souled, dreamless Paul. He grows numb and unloving from his dreary, daily battle with The Man. He flirts with high-yellows. He hates the demanding pain of her childbearing. Finally, for this black Emma Bovary, there is left only a shrunken life of pretzels and beer, of hard-lipped encounters with the whites, a chapterful of queer neighbors, and glimpses of what might have been:

> She watched the little dreams of smoke as they spiraled about his hand, and she thought about happenings. She was afraid to suggest to him that, to most people, nothing at all "happens." That most people merely live from day to day until they die. That, after he had been dead a year, doubtless fewer than five people would think of him oftener than once a year. That there might even come a year when no one on earth would think of him at all. . . .
> I'll never come back, Maud Martha assured herself, when she hung up her apron at eight in the

evening. She knew Mrs. Burns-Cooper would be puzzled. The wages were very good. Indeed, what could be said in explanation? Perhaps that the hours were long. I couldn't explain *my* explanation, she thought. . . . Why, one was a human being. One wore clean nightgowns. One loved one's baby. One drank cocoa by the fire—or the gas range— come the evening, in the wintertime.

It is a powerful, beautiful dagger of a book, a womanly book, as generous as it can possibly be. It teaches more, more quickly, more lastingly, than a thousand pages of protest. It is one answer to Langston Hughes' question: "What happens to a dream deferred?"

There are a number of other Negro novelists of the current and last generations possessed of what one might call "writing-class" talent. Their imaginings (or reminiscences) have a kind of momentary, specious solidity; they can half convince a reader to believe in their characters (if not always to care about them) while reading. But it all flattens back into so many pages of print once the covers of the book are shut.

The common characteristic of these books, books just barely commercial, is a combination of quiet competence —the authors *do* know how to write—and a flat forgettableness. The stories dissolved away too soon, for all the evident care, for all the plot structuring and poetry and rewriting and affection. The recollections are undigested, the creations are incomplete. William Demby's *Beetlecreek* (1950), Pauli Marshall's *Brown Girl, Brownstones* (1959), John A. Williams' *Sissie* (1963), William Kelly's *A Different Drummer* (1963), Ernest Gaines' *Catherine Carmier* (1964): each is well writ-

153

ten, serious of purpose, personal, uniquely imagined. Each, conceivably, might win a small prize. Each casts its new light on the race war. Kelly and Gaines show a sense of dark history and an epic imagination, Kelly a talent for structural play, Demby a rich sense of style, Marshall and Williams a vivid feeling for familial tensions. It is criminally unkind to shelve them here anonymously together—there are certainly bins below *them*, and I can imagine intelligent readers finding much truth and beauty in any one of their books. (It is a question, really, of one's own threshold of imaginative susceptibility.) But I found only ripples, small delights, excitements too quickly gone. These are good novels, by small, skilled men and women, but with no warrant of permanence. They are novels to be softly commended, but not, in good faith, recommended, unless you have oceans of time, are too tired for major works, or have read everything else already.

I should like, as I said, to make a special case for Ann Petry, who may prove in the end to be one of the most useful and important of all. She has written so far three novels, *The Street* (1946), *Country Place* (1947), and *The Narrows* (1953). The first is set, brutally and convincingly, in Harlem. The second two take place in small Connecticut towns like the one where the author was born, towns brutal in their own way, and no less convincing. *The Street* and *The Narrows* are race novels to an important degree; the cast of *Country Place* is almost entirely white.

Mrs. Petry has—this first must be granted—an uncomfortable tendency to contrive sordid plots (as opposed to merely writing of sordid events). She seems to require a "shocking" chain of scandalous doings, secret affairs, family skeletons revealed, brutal crimes, whispered evil, adulterous intrigue on which to cast her creative imagination, in the manner of the great Victorians or the tawdry moderns. So wise is her writing, though, so real are her characters, so total is her sympathy, that one can often accept the faintly cheap horrors and contrivances. Even if not, though, he can dispense with them. It may seem odd to suggest reading a novel while skipping the plot; but it can be done. And if one allows himself to be overexcited by these intrigues (it *is* hard to escape their clutches, but one should), he misses, I think, the real treasures of Ann Petry's fiction.

There is, first, more intelligence in her novels, paragraph for paragraph, than in those of any other writer I have mentioned; solid, earned, tested intelligence. This woman is sharp. Her wisdom is more useful, even, more durable, than the brilliant, diamond-edged acuteness of Gwendolyn Brooks.

This wisdom, secondly, reveals itself in a prose that is rich and crisp, and suavely shot with the metallic threads of irony. It is a style of constant surprise and delight, alive and alight on the page. It is so charged with sense and pleasure you can taste it—and yet never (almost never) is it mere "display."

And out of the female wisdom, the chewy style, grow characters of shape and dimension, people made out of love, with whole histories evoked in a page. There is not one writer in a thousand who owns so genuine and generous and undiscriminating a creative sympathy. Ann Petry *becomes* each character she mentions, grants each one a full, felt intensity of being, the mean and the loving, the white and the black, even when they come

155

and go in only fifty words. Rich sick old ladies, lecher-
ous toads, toddlers, half-animal brutes, the belligerently
independent, the loved and unloved, the passion- and
obsession-maddened, those who scarcely exist: each one,
difficult as it may seem, she enters to become, becomes
to create, with a universality of creative sympathy that
is honestly Shakespearean. (Or at least Faulknerian; he
does it too.)

This, to me, the intelligence, the style, and above all
the creative sympathy, is what sets Ann Petry apart
among this second rank of American Negro novelists,
sets her, in fact, into a place almost as prominent and
promising as that of the bigger three. She is not, of
course, writing "about" the race war, any more than
most of the last eight or ten novelists mentioned are.
This is a delusion fostered either by publishers, playing
up a profitable approach, or by the fake guilty egocen-
tricity of white readers, who presume that all books by
Negroes must somehow be about them. But if an American Negro can, despite all, develop such an understanding of other people as Ann Petry's—and more prodigious still, *convey* that understanding—then let her
write what *Peyton Place*-plots she will, she is working
toward a genuine truce in the war.

Even as I write this, seven more novels and books of
stories by American Negroes are announced for publication. These remarks will be dated very soon. Men
go on writing and writing, and American Negroes, for
all their enforced illiteracy, have more to say than most.
But one must stop somewhere. This much will keep the
willing white reader busy for some while. It may, in the
long run, contribute to his own Emancipation.

VIII
CONCLUSIONS

If nothing else, this brief survey should make clear the ample and diverse range of the American Negro's literature in the last twenty-five years, let alone the last hundred-plus. Recollection of this variety, in fact, may help check the reader's tendency to think too exclusively in terms of "the Negro writer" or "the Negro experience." Too much of this essay already has fostered this tendency to dehumanize and stereotype—all the more reason that the generalizations of the first chapter should be tested against the particulars of the others.

There is, obviously, no "Negro experience" in America, though some Negro polemicists among our authors may try to make one think so. There are twenty million separate experiences. To take every Negro author, foolish or wise, as a spokesman for the Negro is absurd. It is simply to foster the lumping dehumanization, the stereotyping that has been one of the race's most frustrating debasements. If sophisticated white Americans (and Europeans) have outgrown the singing-and-dancing-fool concept of the Negro, they have not learned a great deal in the process if they now rush to adopt each Negro novelist's new agonized, hate-filled hero as the norm. There may be, realistically speaking, some minimal unity of experience and heritage partaken in by great numbers of American Negroes, although what Lena Horne has in common with an Alabama tenant farmer must be so small as to dissolve into the metaphysical. But to presume anything further, to make any generalization for the Negro race on the basis of these works without the most scrupulous qualification, is to debase new knowledge into something worse than ignorance, to fall back on the We-They simplifications that prolong the war.

All sociological or "race-psychological" interpretations of literature are to some degree illicit, insofar as they discard the essential element of the author's private experience. They must be conducted with exceptional delicacy, with constant reservations, with an implicit confession of their partial, tentative, and fictional nature. All this granted, what can one learn, if not of The American Negro, then of American Negroes from the literature surveyed?

One can learn, first, a great deal about the quality of life in the urban ghettoes of the North, in particular those of Harlem and Chicago's South Side. (Our picture of Negro life in the rural or village South today, on the other hand, is dim and distorted. Decreasing numbers of this generation of Negro authors know it firsthand.) One comes to know the crumbling, smelly tenements with their rats and roaches and garbagey, urinous halls; the ubiquitous rent men and numbers runners; the elaborate underground codes of dress and conversation and behavior. In this dismal world, where the only legal jobs open are maid or scrub woman or kitchen help, shoeshine boy, porter, elevator operator, day laborer, or bellboy, the reader is seized with the awareness of a life style so barbarically limited that its only comforts are alcohol, crime, dope, and, especially, sex and religion.

It is clear that sex, for better or worse, becomes something quite open and unashamed, something un-American, in the straitened conditions of the ghetto. The slum-dwelling Negro child is fully and frankly aware of casual sex, of bastardy, of the various manifestations of human depravity to a degree unimaginable by most carefully cushioned white puritans. It seems further clear, however, that most "upstanding," illiberal Negro citizens are as (publicly) unenthusiastic about inter-racial sex as their paler-faced counterparts.

The fervid, evangelical variety of Negro Christianity ("a fairly desperate emotional business," according to Baldwin) has produced a marvelous subliterature all its own. It has dominated Negro writing from the anony-mous spirituals and the poems of James Weldon John-son to the Harlem store-front congregation stories by Baldwin and Hughes. Tour-de-force imitations of the Negro preacher's sermon abound in American Negro writing, an incantatory progression of Scriptural echoes and images, moving through an associative emotional crescendo. The elaborate Negro funeral is a stock-in-trade setting. There is no question, despite Wright's militant atheism and Baldwin's recantation, of the still dominant place of religion in many Negro lives.

Beyond this, the white reader acquires a great deal of inside information about Negro life, of the sort I con-sidered in Chapter III. The obsession, for example, with shades of darkness as an index of acceptability continues to torment scores of characters, even in the "freer" liter-ature of the past generation. It is the high-yellow or ivory-beige girls who are always the more desired; a few are even light enough to "pass," which shows where the values come from. Similar is the concern for "good" hair, which writers like John A. Williams have at-tacked. Langston Hughes writes in his memoirs of

159

A'lelia Walker, a Gatsby-like party giver of the twenties, who inherited millions from "the pride and glory of the Negro race," Madame Walker's Hair-Straightening Formula.

The Negro caste system, one learns from these works, is elaborate and unique. At the top (not counting international-class athletes and entertainers) is the small group of professional positions still open to the Negro in America—doctors, dentists, and lawyers to the Negro community; undertakers, burial-society and insurance agents; preachers, barbers, and beauticians. One learns something, too, of the Negro Establishment—of the colleges and professors, the organizations and their leaders, the potent Negro press, a Society with its own debutante balls; of the *Amsterdam News*, *Ebony*, the Theresa Hotel Smart Set.

One learns much, too, of the aggressive enmity of Black against Black. "Assimilationists" fight with Black Nationalists of various breeds—Purlie Victorious with his "ten thousand Queens of Sheba," Assagai of *A Raisin in the Sun*, Ras the Destroyer from *Invisible Man*. Defenders of Booker T. Washington fight the partisans of W. E. B. DuBois. Angry young black men, usually author surrogates, curse the realists, the accommodationists—the Uncle Toms, the White Men's Niggers, the dickty Sugar Hill bourgeoisie with its downtown tastes and manners (and hair). The despised and distrusted Negro Leaders—the term is meant to suggest a white-approved, self-serving type of leader in the Booker Washington tradition, like Ellison's magnificent Dr. Bledsoe, President Wimbush of Redding's *Stranger and Alone*—come in for particular abuse.

At a more urgent level, the white observer is taught

160

a good deal about what Richard Wright called, coolly and acutely, "the ethics of living Jim Crow." There is perhaps no Negro character in the recent works discussed in this survey except Walker Vessels, the gunman in *The Slave*, and Richard Henry in *Blues for Mister Charlie* who is not forced at some time to adopt the degrading role of "nigger" before white men. To get a job, to avoid arrest, to ward off a blow, to buy a ticket, to beg charity or mercy or even justice, the Negro character must forever cringe and grin and play the ignominious part invented for him by white Americans. Some (the Negro Leaders, the operators, the professional Uncle Toms: Gitlow in *Purlie Victorious*) so perfect their acting as to capitalize on it.

A Negro learns to gauge precisely what reaction the alien person facing him desires, and he produces it with disarming artlessness.
(James Baldwin, *Notes of a Native Son*)

Others derive compensation from the useful wedge of moral superiority they achieve over the harassed, blustering whites, who never know when Negroes are acting and when they are not.

Other aspects of peculiarly "racial" psychology are dramatized and discussed as well. The first childhood discovery of one's "inferior" racial status often assumes the stature of a traumatic event. "Race men," Negroes who impulsively "talk race," are regarded in their own society as unhealthy. The more doctrinaire varieties of race men consider hatred of whites as a categorical imperative, as useful as it is necessary. Race pride is encouraged or mocked, depending on one's cynical temperature. Among the lower orders and the populist

161

poets, Joe Louis and Louis Armstrong and Negro History Week and the African heritage may be very important; to the rising black bourgeoisie, jazz and sweet potatoes and all things "Negro" are to be avoided at all possible costs. The existentialist hero and his contemporary creator may scorn them both, but still find a home with Miles Davis and the "authentic" Bessie Smith blues.

At the deepest, most fundamental level, one can note certain psychological obsessions, certain fixations, certain recurring myths that loom very large in Negro literature. Here we are dealing with indirect communication. What one learns is what he intuits and interprets from certain constantly repeated types and patterns, certain ritual events in the writings of American Negroes. It is not important at this level whether or not the myths are true in fact. It *is* important that they seem to be necessary.

One is the myth of Negro endurance I have referred to, a supposed racial duty or trait of Going On Nevertheless, exemplified in the bitter affirmations of the blues and in many Negro poems, or in the work of Langston Hughes. Related to this is the mythical figure of the Negro Mammy or Grandma, all bosom and lap and folk wisdom and stability—Faulkner's Dilsey (*The Sound and the Fury*) is the classic representative, or Ethel Waters on stage or screen. Ellison's Mary, Hughes' Aunt Hager, Lorraine Hansberry's Mama, many others maintain the tradition in Negro writing—a counterpart figure to the lost and angry male.

American Negroes would seem, from this sampling, to be as obsessed by interracial sex myths as stupid Southern white men are supposed to be. More interest-

162

ingly, they seem to be obsessed by white men's versions of the myths. The whole issue is darkly confusing, but it is astonishing how often Negro authors feel compelled to create scenes in which their heroes are purposely tempted by white women; or by white men *using* their own women to tempt; or scenes of white men who try to force or fake an interracial rape, who put the black hero up to it, compel him to it, and then accuse him of the deed whether he accomplishes it or not. Now, white men may well do such things, or want to do them, for heaven knows what reasons of racial-sexual insecurity. Interracial rape is the South's great symbolic sin, its unspeakable desire (and "The spirit of the South is the spirit of America," according to James Baldwin). It is the professed occasion of two thousand lynchings and the obvious occasion of many millions of brown Negroes. But why Negro writers should want to dramatize this sordid white desire is not altogether clear.

Similar to this is the use by Negro writers of white men's abuse; many seem to enjoy "playing white men," and cursing out their "nigger" heroes with obscene and excessive abandon. The use of murder as the symbolic act, for a final example, is also fairly frequent: murder, *real* murder, by Negro of white as a kind of alternative to love—as if it were the only possible honest communication between the races. This is all distinctly race-war material. As to what, specifically, it may signify, although I have my theories like anyone else, I am incompetent to speculate in print.

Finally, this reading can be for the white reader an education in the history and folklore, the suffering and dreams of American Negroes. What one gains will be in direct measure to his ignorance at the start: the story of the slave ships, the character of the American police, and the intraracial Negro codes were among my lessons. It could all have been acquired, I suppose, from the vast library of non-fictional texts about the Negro in America; but this, for me, was a livelier, a less forgettable way to learn.

This, then, is a glimpse of what one can learn from the writings of American Negroes. And as there is no one "Negro experience," there is also, obviously, no "Negro writer." Most writers who are Negroes hate the deindividuation, the "Groupthink" such essays as this propose (though they themselves—e.g., Negro writers' conferences, etc.—are among the first to use the category). Most writers of any breed would despise it—a writer is by definition a solitary being. Everything one says about "the Negro writer" is false to some degree. There are personalities subtle and obvious, mean and magnanimous, imaginative and dense, narrow and far-seeing, self-deluded and self-aware among Negro writers, just as there are among all manner of human beings. There are stunted, clumsy, crayon-scrawl "artists" with their primitive morality-play stories. There are untrained and undisciplined scandal-drooling naturalists. There are many non-thinkers. The range of possibility includes Ellison and Brooks; and Willard Motley, Baldwin at his best, and Baldwin at his worst. Literary history is too full already of formulaic generalizations about groups of writers for us to add any more about Negroes.

And yet, and yet—a few conclusions, a very few, may be drawn about "the Negro writer" in America, present and future. He *is* different, both because he is black and because he is a writer. "His" experience has been different—both from that of the white writers and from that of his non-writing fellows.

As an American writer, first of all, he will be, of course, lonely and introverted. He will be misunderstood by other people (black and white), misread by critics, harassed or unappreciated by his publishers, and bragged about by his mother. He will feel, much of the time, cut off from other men. As a Negro, he may blame this on his color; but it is only the condition of most serious American writers. His heroes are likely to be egotists like himself, "strangers and alone"; their Negroness may only symbolize or intensify *his* dilemma as a writer. The ranks of Negro authors, like the ranks of white authors, will have their quota of "first novelists," of family-thwarted, college-bred, sexually insecure solipsists who feel driven to make books out of their own unimportant stories and fantasies. They should be taken no more seriously for being Negro. A Negro author *will* be, of course, atypical of his race; there is something very "white middle class" in the very notion of wanting to publish a book. The profession of writing (whether practiced full or part time, whether remunerative or not) is by definition cerebral, Western, leisured, and leisure-class oriented. All Negroes who do not write, even relatives and friends, are going to seem alien to a Negro who does.

The Negro writer, moreover—especially the novelist—stands the same risk as every other American writer of losing his openness and honesty, the more a professional he becomes; of losing his original purpose and identity; of turning from writer to Writer. His first book, let us say, is done: *Native Son, Invisible Man, Go*

165

Tell It on the Mountain. Gradually, he becomes a Commodity, then a Celebrity; he attends press parties, signs autographs, reads from his works, participates in college symposia (on the Negro), gives largely of his Opinions, talks literary gossip, writes about writers (Ellison on Wright, Baldwin on Mailer).

It can happen to anyone, and there is reason in their last or latest works to fear that it has happened to each of America's three leading Negro novelists. The Negro writer may be no *more* susceptible than the white, but he is no less.

But as a writer who is also a Negro, he may have special problems as well, obstacles to overcome that no white writer will ever know. The problems, moreover, are rarely those discussed at Negro writers' conferences: whether to identify with America or Africa, whether to write of Negroes or whites, for what audience he should write, his place in the democratic myth, the nature of America, *négritude*, and so forth. The man to whom such questions are real questions is probably more a *conférencier* than a writer.

Consider: how many Negro authors have ever been able to create, alive from within, a convincing, living white man—except as a ritual, negative self-projection, or a crude stick figure? Some, perhaps: Baldwin, Ann Petry. How many, to take it further, have created *any* person, black or white, wholly other than themselves? Ann Petry again, Owen Dodson in his Deaconess Quick; a few others. Consider then, the central place of autobiography in Negro literature. Richard Wright's and Katherine Dunham's are small classics. James Weldon Johnson's, Langston Hughes', and Saunders Redding's are all richly full, and readable. The most recent—

Claude Brown's, Horace Cayton's, Malcolm X's—are among the most moving of all. But there are scores of others, and more coming out every year: *every* Negro who achieves the most marginal degree of fame feels compelled to tell his story, however little it may differ from the next man's. This autobiographical insistence, this locked-in-the-self imprisonment, suggests that, for most American Negroes, the day of artistic objectivity and detachment has not yet arrived. (The finest, most understanding piece of race war literature ever written —*A Passage to India*—was composed by an upper class Englishman in 1924.) Just how many Negro imaginations, given the environmental limits of American prejudice, *can* make the break and soar free? Or have their owners perhaps other, more necessary things to do first?

The Negro writer may feel, honestly and honorably, that he has quite a number of tasks to fulfill that a white writer would never dream of: a deal of seeking, searching, puzzling out answers about himself, of ritual attacking and exorcising. There is still, he may vividly feel, a war on.

From this racial war that is America most white writers, even Southern white writers, can opt out; that is the privilege of the comfortably more powerful combatant. For the embattled underdog, it is not so easy, even if he is a pacifist at heart. He may feel obliged, like some demon-driven character out of Faulkner, to talk about his history, his sufferings, his burden, to play over and over his oppressively limited range of theme.

These may be for him ritual stages, psychologically or sociologically necessary, that must be gotten through. The Negro writer has, in addition to every writer's burden of mother, father, frustrations, nightmares, and

167

shames, burdens all of his own, imposed by America, that he has to deal with or be dishonest—which is to say, or not be a writer. (All things considered, it is astonishing not that there are so *few* Negro writers in the United States, but so many.)

He *may* still overcome them. Some already have, to quiet degrees. One Negro (two, three) may soon come to terms with himself, with his undefinable, unbalanced, senseless American "place"; and then find himself able to sit down and concentrate on something more objective than his own unfortunate story.

We will then, I hope, have less of the frenzied war literature, the now necessary dramatizations of The Problem, with their apocalyptic insistence on the ritual battling of Black vs. White, of We vs. They; and more unfrenzied, sympathetic renderings of the total life of non-militant, non-warring Americans who happen to be Negroes. It would help us all. The great Irish writers, for a precedent, oppressed, militant, suffering, did themselves and their readers immortal service in defining so completely the life style, the inner necessity of their people.

But most Negroes—including most Negro writers— seem still to be too uncertain of, too unhappy about their own racial identity to be able to celebrate the Life of their People. Many still half-want to deny their people (which is understandable, when the majority despises them), to become white, in fact, to adopt white values, to "assimilate." So they cannot, will not write of Negro life *except* as a war against the envied and hated white majority. It is one thing to want to be free; it is quite another, and sick, to want to be a different color. It makes for neurosis, not for art. But America, all of it, goes on hating blackness, fosters the neurosis, and holds off the day of a true Negro art.

But if no Negro yet has achieved sufficient stability and content to write fully and comfortably of Negro life, this is no reason to conclude that none will. Faulkner had, at least, ambivalent feelings about the South, but yet was able to become, sympathetically, a whole world full of Southerners.

Still, Faulkner was not consciously waging a hopeless war. He was relatively content with what he was. He did not, one assumes, have to go on night and day fighting the battle of himself. The Dostoevskys and Joyces and Bellows and Faulkners are (were) *pleased*, one infers, to be Russian and Irish and Jewish and Southern American. It seems almost insanely difficult for a Negro in America to come to this stage of self-acceptance, self-contentment. Ralph Ellison protests that *he* has; but his protest is so exceptional that one tends (unfairly) to doubt.

Ideally, I think he will come, a Negro pleased to be a Negro in America, despite all; one willing to love, live, and recreate for the world the lives of his people. It is a stirring thought that one man could affect the necessary self-redefinition for millions of people, the acceptance of a racial identity.

Then—and only then—after that as yet unreached stage is attained, we can hope, after perhaps another generation, for a Negro writer who can turn his sympathies outward, and acquire an understanding of suffering whites or Orientals, people everywhere; a man who can reach out and know by sympathy the sufferings of others, possessed (like the mythical twentieth-century Jew) of a unique and world-wide sympathy for suffering, for the inner frustrations of all manner of men. He, this unborn Negro writer, may teach the rest of America—James Baldwin has served, after all, as a crude, first-stage national conscience—what suffering, endurance, uncertainty, desperation, fury, communal understanding, and pity are like. Like the American Jew, he may retain of his racial identity then little more than an impulsive sense of universal moral justice.

As some men are bettered by oppression, so the real humanists of a future America, Richard Wright predicted (in *White Man, Listen!*), will be the Negroes who can love. As the American Dilemma makes clear, the Negro is already far freer of psychological burdens than his puzzled white master, and will be far readier to assume the role of national conscience, "after the war."

To sum up: we wait, still, for a Negro writer who can tell us, truly, what it is like to be a Negro. But they have other things to do, first: they have a war to fight. The Jews became no one's conscience-dictators until after Hitler, who came after more than a thousand years of only slightly less holocaustic and dehumanizing oppression. American Negro writers must first find themselves, and rest content with what they find, before they can tell us about it—or about ourselves.

INDEX

171

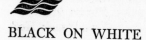

BLACK ON WHITE

The text has been composed on the Linotype in Monticello. The display type is Torino.

The book is printed by letterpress on Warren's No. 66 Antique paper.

Composed, printed and bound by H. Wolff Book Mfg. Co.

DESIGNED BY CATHRYN S. AISON